Med...
People Who Worry

1/15

Meditations for
People Who Worry

Anne Wilson Schaef

BALLANTINE WELLSPRING
THE BALLANTINE PUBLISHING GROUP   NEW YORK

A Ballantine Wellspring Book
Published by The Ballantine Publishing Group

Copyright © 1996 by Anne Wilson Schaef

www.randomhouse.com/BB

Library of Congress Cataloging-in-Publication Data
Meditations for people who (may) worry too much /
[compiled by] Anne Wilson Schaef.—1st ed.
p.   cm.
ISBN 0-345-39406-2
1. Worry—Religious aspects—Christianity.   2. Devotional calendars.
I. Schaef, Anne Wilson.
BV4908.5.M36   1996
158'.12—dc20   96-13685

Cover design by Min Choi
Cover illustration by Mary Flock
Text design by Holly Johnson

Manufactured in the United States of America

First Edition: May 1996

10   9   8   7   6   5

Acknowledgments

There are some people who have been especially helpful in gathering and sharing quotes and I want to mention them here. Karen Martin and Betsy Martin gathered quotes from friends. Pete Sidley, Connie Lee Anderson-Brown, and Dolly Toombs generously added new quotes and ideas. The Living in Process Network internationally shared quotes and ideas and sent in material. Barbara Moulton at Harper San Francisco generously sent me a book she had edited to help me in my search for new ideas.

I especially want to mention Chuck Tesmer and Pete Sidley, whose love and support—and ideas—were always there. Pete Sidley in the Wilson-Schaef Associates, Inc., office took on the mammoth task of putting my yellow tablet pages in the computer, checking quotes, editing, interacting with the publisher, getting the permissions and, in general, shepherding this book through the process.

Of course, no acknowledgments would ever be complete without recognizing the unqualified support of my son, Roddy, who is always back there yelling, "Yeah, Mom!" (which he did at a very solemn moment when I was given an Honorary Doctorate at Kenyon College a few years ago!).

Jonathan Lazear, Wendy Lazear, and all the people at the Lazear Agency have always supported my ideas and my work. And, I am grateful for my editor,

Cheryl Woodruff, and my new publisher, Ballantine, for the possibilities to continue to put my books and my ideas "out there."

I am so grateful for the people in my life. I feel so blessed. And I am also grateful for the Creator who works through me when I have enough sense to get out of the way.

Introduction

Never, in a million years, could we have predicted the national and international success of *Meditations for Women Who Do Too Much*. True, it had a great title (and I had to fight over the title) which "hit a nerve" in American women and women around the world. Yet, I do not believe that the title alone could have made that book the million-plus international bestseller it is today. I have received so many letters from women the world over stating how helpful this book has been and what a daily companion it has become. I feel especially gratified about this response because this little book represents the first time I ventured forth with my philosophy of life and the way of living I am teaching in the Living in Process work. My previous books were more focused upon my observations of the world around me, with hints of my personal philosophy. In *Meditations for Women Who Do Too Much*, I put my beliefs on the line and they resonated.

I had thought of writing a sequel, *Meditations for Women Who Are Recovering from Doing Too Much*. Yet, I wanted to get on with something new (I'm an Aries).

Then I sat down and thought, What else do people in this culture do that robs them of their ability to be fully alive as much as doing too much does? Then it hit me—worry. Worry is a national and an international pastime. Yet, no worrier wants to worry about whether or not they worry *too* much. Somehow, worrying doesn't

Worry

*It is estimated that more than thirteen million
American adults are chronic worriers. The
National Institute of Mental Health says anxiety
disorders are America's most commonly reported
mental-health problems.*

AMY H. BERGER

My goodness. Do you think that this means thirteen
million people need this book? I hope so!

Seriously, though, we seem to have developed an
epidemic and we don't even know it. Almost everyone
seems to worry about something and, yet, we rarely talk
about worry as a problem. Maybe that is because worry
is so integrated into the way we have come to live and
be in the world that we don't even notice it.

There are many facets to worry. Worry is not simple
nor is it simply addressed. We could worry about worry
and then worry about our worrying about worry. But,
why chase our tails.

Clearly, we need to explore worry, we need to understand worry, we need to share experiences and wisdom about worry. And, most of all, we need some relief
from worry. It's a new year and we have 366 daily meditations to feed and heal us.

**There's a certain solace in knowing that I am not alone:
I have thirteen million worriers to keep me company.**

Normal May Not Be Natural

Worrying is the most natural and spontaneous of all human functions. It is time to acknowledge this, perhaps even to learn to do it better.

LEWIS THOMAS

A school for worriers, what an idea! Registrations would soar. Yet, most of us have already had years of training in our homes, our churches, and especially in our schools and universities. What have we come to as a civilization when we see worry as "natural and spontaneous" when it is actually cultivated every day by our culture.

In a society based on the illusion of control, I am sure that there is some truth to the statement that worry is "the most natural and spontaneous of all human functions," and just because worry has become the norm does not mean that it is "natural."

We need to distinguish between what is "natural" and what is "normal," remembering that normal may not be healthy in a dysfunctional situation.

Surprises/Control

What we anticipate seldom occurs, what we least expected generally happens.

BENJAMIN DISRAELI

Surprises! What a wonder they are. I have lived long enough to be able to look back on my life and see the times when I believed that my life was just perfect and all I wanted to do was to stop everything and keep it that way—no surprises—just constant, consistent, dependable perfection!

How lucky I was that I did not have that kind of power! I would have missed so much.

Our dislike of surprises is in direct proportion to our illusion of control.

The "least expected" is the real test of our "true mettle."

Being Creators Not Victims

*The natural role of twentieth-century man is
anxiety.*

NORMAN MAILER

If anxiety has truly become natural, maybe this should
be a clue that it is time to do something differently as
we approach the twenty-first century.

I, for one, do not believe the Creator had a constant state of anxiety in mind for us as human beings.
We have designed our lives and our societies in such a
way as to make anxiety our reality.

What good news! If we are the ones who have designed our lives and society—constructed the sets and
created the drama—then we also have the power to
change them.

**We are not just the victims of our situation. We are
the creators of something new.**

Peace

Holy Mother Earth, the trees and all nature, are
witness to your thoughts and deeds.

WINNEBAGO

Peace—I feel peace when I read this.

I have an old American Indian Elder friend and he repeatedly has said to me, "When you are sick and broken, return to your Mother, the earth. Put your head against her breast and she will heal you."

I have to quiet down to do this. I have to stop what I am doing, go into nature and sit upon the earth. When I stretch out upon the earth and let my entire body relax upon her, I do feel better.

Sometimes, I even go to a favorite tree and lean against her, taking the time to stay there until I feel better.

How marvelous it would be if all our thoughts and deeds were worthy to be witnessed by "the trees and all nature."

Worry, Work, and Creativity

*The reason why worry kills more people than
work is that more people worry than work.*

ROBERT FROST

Of course, the best recipe for an early demise is a creative combination of work and worry. Since work is one of the favorite preoccupations of worriers and worry about work is one of the avenues to overwork, the two actually result in an electrifying and truly self-supporting (so to speak) relationship.

How creative we are in working out lethal relationships in our lives!

Robert Frost used his creativity differently. He not only wrote poems that were simple, yet profound, he was able to take simple observations and, with "tongue in cheek," call our awareness to complex issues. This is true creativity.

If I worry about how to work and worry more creatively—I've probably missed the point.

Gossip

Love and scandal are the best sweeteners of tea.
HENRY FIELDING

Ah, afternoon tea! How delicious it is to take a break, leisurely sit with friends, and—gossip.

Now, I happen to think gossip has taken a bum rap in this culture. I tend to think of gossip as a good way for friends to keep informed and for news to be shared among a larger group of people than would otherwise hear about it—and, of course, I want to know about my friends and I want them to know about me.

There are just two important things to remember about gossip for it to be caring and not harmful to the gossiper or gossipee. First, we need to be willing to repeat whatever we are saying directly to the person *and do it.*

And, second, there has to be absolutely no judgmentalism in it. If we are not clear on these two points, then we'd better keep our mouths shut.

See how important it is to be clear. If we're not, we are apt to miss much "sweet" information about love and scandal.

Goodness

*Goodness is uneventful. It does not flash, it
glows.*

DAVID GRAYSON

We don't hear a lot about goodness these days. Often
goodness is uneventful. It creeps up on us slowly, like a
coral sunset at the end of a long day. Goodness is as
simple as a neighbor I hadn't yet met sending over a loaf
of freshly baked bread after I had an accident.

Goodness doesn't get much press. There's no adrenaline, no conflict, no excitement—none of the urges we
have learned to feed upon that tell us we are alive.

Goodness is everyday. It is noticing—noticing a
new dress, noticing pain, noticing when someone is not
being honest.

Goodness is the gentleness that makes loving
others a process and not an event.

**Goodness is never out of style. And, we often have to
slow down to see and experience it in ourselves and in
others.**

Action

I can spend hours of worrying about what might be in some years when I am older. I really can get depressed. If I would collect all these hours and simply do what I have to do today, my supply of work would vanish and I wouldn't have enough left over for my work addiction. Worrying keeps me from doing what I love to do and feeds my addictions.

URSULA

When we think of worry not as an activity but as a "filler," we have a totally different perspective on it. We can use it to avoid and fill. How convenient!

It is interesting to think about worry keeping us from what we have to do and feeding our addictions. I have often heard it said that one of the major reasons the Twelve Step program of Alcoholics Anonymous works is that it is a program of action. How much safer it is to think about things than it is to do them.

Perhaps the first step is to forgive ourselves for our inactivity, and then get up and do something—for someone else.

What might be always robs us of what is!

Anxiety

*Every little yielding to anxiety is a step away from
the natural heart of man.*

JAPANESE PROVERB

The "natural heart of man" is buried deep in all of us.
That heartbeat tells us that we are alive and we have the
opportunity to live this gift of life each and every day.
We have the possibility to be as fully human as we can
be and to experience what being fully human means.

Our anxieties, our fears, our need to control, and
our dishonesties all rob us of the human heart connection that allows us to live the life we can. We cannot
stop these feelings. They are human. We all have them.
They are there for a reason, and it is important for us to
notice them and see what we can learn from them. Yet,
yielding to them or indulging in them is only a loss to
ourselves and to those around us.

**When I open the floodgates of anxiety and fear and
"yield," I stay stuck. When I notice and stay open to
my learnings, I nourish my "natural heart."**

Thinking

I've been sober long enough to know not to trust anything I think.

ANONYMOUS

I love this statement. My mind is not always reliable nor is it always my friend. This is especially true when I do not balance it out with my heart and my feelings and my intuition. Also, my mind is not my friend when I lead with it. It does a much better job for me when I lead with my feelings and intuition and then take all this information into my brain for final processing.

There's nothing wrong with thinking. Our ability to think is a gift and when we use it well, it is our friend. We tend to get into trouble when we start to believe that our thoughts, our interpretations, and our constructs are real and we act accordingly.

When I start mistrusting what I think, I am moving from information to wisdom.

- Mind as a tool. A Computer.
- A servant of your heart.
- Sometimes spits out bad data.
- Must Use Intuition
- For "Study" only
- Mentally strong to turn off & on.

Faith

Behold the fowls of the air: for they sow not,
neither do they reap, nor gather into barns; yet
your heavenly Father feedeth them. Are ye not
much better than they? Which of you by taking
thought can add one cubit unto his stature? And
why take ye thought for raiment? Consider the
lilies of the field, how they grow; they toil not,
neither do they spin:

And yet I say unto you, That even Solomon
in all his glory was not arrayed like one of these.

Wherefore, if God so clothe the grass of the
field, which today is, and tomorrow is cast into the
oven, shall he not much more clothe you, O ye of
little faith?

Therefore take no thought, saying, What shall
we eat? or What shall we drink? or Wherewithal
shall we be clothed?

MATTHEW 6:26–31, THE BIBLE

As a child I was drawn to this Bible passage and fascinated with it. It seemed both impossible and true, and I never could reconcile the two.

I now see that I was stuck in a childish dualism of do nothing and be taken care of—or live in faith and starve. God has never expected us to do nothing! We have to do our footwork and then have faith. Ultimately, we have to trust what the Creator has in mind for us.

Living a life of faith is not passive or lazy. It is doing the best we can and then letting go.

Information

Ala i ka 'opua ke ola: he ola nui, he ola laula, he ola hohonu, he ola ki 'eki 'e.

Life is in the clouds; great life, broad life, deep life, elevated life. [The reader of omens knows rain and prosperity or warns of disaster.]

HAWAIIAN PROVERB

For the last several years, I have been spending time with Native people and Native Elders throughout the world. I never cease to be amazed with the vast sources of their information. Their hearts, their guts, and their ancestors are all there broadcasting information. The clouds, the trees, the birds, the animals, the fish, and the insects all add their part.

How rich are the possibilities when we use all of our senses to gather information about the world.

No wonder we get anxious. We aren't operating with all the information.

Needs

*Putting out what I need when it may not be what
other people need is very hard for me.*

RAE

Saying what we need is not easy for a lot of us. It is even
more difficult when what we need is not what other
people need. It is even *more* difficult when our needs
conflict with what other people need. Yet, saying what
we need is one of the ways we have of respecting ourselves and respecting others.

We respect ourselves when we recognize that we
have needs and we have the right to have needs. We
may not always be able to get our needs met and that's
okay. We will never have a chance of getting our needs
met if we don't acknowledge that we have needs and
say so.

We respect others by saying what we need because
in so doing we let them know who we are and we offer
the glorious possibility of being intimate. How disrespectful of others it is—especially those who are important to us—not to offer them these opportunities.

**Letting others know what I need may be one of life's
most respectful acts.**

Our Bodies

Worry affects circulation, the heart and the glands, the whole nervous system, and profoundly affects the heart. I have never known a man who died from overwork, but many who died from doubt.

CHARLES H. MAYO

This is an old quotation, yet it is so timely. While we have begun to recognize the danger of workaholism and stress and how lethal these activities are, we still seem to be in denial about the roles that worry and doubt play in our lives.

Worry and doubt are not just harmless activities of the mind. They affect our bodies and their ability to function.

The human heart of a worrier has no home because the fast-beating heart of a worrier believes in control and takes on superhuman responsibility—believes in the ability to control everything in that life. This kind of control is a big order. In fact, it is an impossible order and the body often, upon realizing this, explodes.

I have a wonderful body. It performs well when I ask it to do what it is humanly capable of doing.

Humor

I'm always afraid I'll wake up one day and find
myself turned serious.

EILEEN

Now, this could be a real problem. I suppose no matter
who we are, where we live, or what kind of work we do,
there is always the dangerous possibility of waking up
one morning and finding ourselves "turned serious."

Turning serious can be deadly. When we lose our
sense of humor, we lose our perspective on life. Without
humor, we can easily confuse reality and begin to think
that we are the center of the universe and that what
happens to us will, indeed, change the course of human
events.

When we "turn serious" we forget that life goes on
and what looked like a disaster last year may have been
exactly the kick we needed to change directions and re-
think where we are going and how we have been.

I suppose I could worry about "turning serious" but if
I did, I would have already done it.

Bad Moods

Worst news for the "Don't Worry, Be Happy"
crowd:

Average number of days each year that an
American is in a bad mood: 110.

Percentage of Americans who are in a good
mood every day: 2.

QUOTED FROM HARPER'S INDEX IN
SUNDAY PARADE MAGAZINE

Now, these are very interesting statistics (let's face it—not all statistics *are* interesting).

Can you believe it? Americans are in a bad mood almost one-third of the time. In order to get a statistic like this (an average), a lot of people have to be in bad moods most of the time. This means, then, that the likelihood of being growled at in the supermarket or snapped at by family or friends is pretty high. This also means that all those people who seem to hate me, not like me, or just disapprove of me may be in a bad mood. There is also the possibility, perhaps, that their bad mood may have nothing to do with me.

Given all the above statistical possibilities, I may just
as well join the two percent of Americans who are in a
good mood. At least we're a small, elite group.

Trust

When I have an investment in the outcome, I am
insulting God.

ANNE WILSON SCHAEF

Sometimes it's difficult to remember that we may just
not know what would be good for us in a certain situation or what might be the best outcome of that situation.

We don't set out to insult God. In fact, insulting
God may be the furthest thing from our minds. Yet,
most of us, most of the time, slip into the arrogant belief
that we know how things should turn out.

We believe we know what is best for our children
and who they should be and what they should do
when they grow up. Sometimes, if we get completely
mad, we believe we know what kind of mate would be
best for them.

And what about work? How easy it is to fall under
the delusion that we know the direction that our career
or our business must take and can make it happen. How
exhausting it is to insult God!

When I do the best I can and then let go of the out-
come, I am trusting God.

Constant Crisis

My folks worried a lot about the cold war. I remember very clearly their fear during the Cuban Missile Crisis. Carrying on the tradition for the next twenty-five years, I couldn't see a contrail high overhead without thinking it might drop the bomb. I'd often imagine quite vividly the big final flash as my city, family, and friends went up in flames. It's how I assumed I'd die and it provided an endless and reliable source of worry for many years. Imagine my surprise when I got into recovery and the cold war ended.

PAUL

The Soviet Union was such an excellent focus for Americans' worry for so many years. When the cold war ended and the Soviet Union began to disintegrate, many people felt lost and ungrounded. There actually had seemed to be something grounding about a collective worry.

When we look outside ourselves for our identity and our reason for existence, it is important to feel we belong.

We have been programmed to look outside ourselves for the reasons we are the way we are. Our preoccupation with events and forces outside ourselves has robbed us of our strength and our identity.

My worry will not change the course of events. I am the only person I can change.

Dishonesty

Excuses doctors and physical therapists have heard
as to why people can't exercise:
- *An earthquake drained my pool.*
- *My dog ate my running shoes.*
- *I can't exercise because of the grizzly bear*
  (heard near a popular walking path in
  Anchorage, Alaska).
- *My wife would be angry with me if I lost*
  weight.
- *If I exercise I might not have enough energy left*
  over for sex.

QUOTED FROM "THE PHYSICIAN &
SPORTSMEDICINE" IN
MEN'S HEALTH

Sometimes we use our worries to avoid doing what we
don't want to do. Somehow it seems much more legiti-
mate if we have a *reason* to hide behind. Our worrying
gives us a way to avoid being honest with ourselves and
others, yet, try as we may, no one is really fooled.

Unfortunately, when we try to deceive others, we
end up erasing little parts of ourselves.

Being lazy is probably not as hard on us as being
dishonest.

Drama

I resent it when life impinges upon my drama.

RIK

Ah, drama! How much of our time we spend running on the fuel of crisis and chaos. There's nothing like an adrenaline hit to give us the illusion of being alive. Often, we get so involved in our dramas that they become more real than life itself. And, we can dramatize anything.

We have an accident and it becomes enlarged with the telling, scarcely recognizable to its original form. Or, we get an illness and life becomes the drama of the illness. Each new phase of the illness brings a new crisis. Or, life happens and for us this happening is not enough. We have to embellish it with a crisis for every event.

Life is a process. It happens. It unfolds. It is up to us what we do with it.

I knew that I was becoming more spiritually grounded when I could no longer "whip up" a crisis no matter what happened.

Good/Negativity

When an unpleasant event occurs unexpectedly, people comment on the fact that at least one did not have to WORRY about that event.

BETSY MARTIN

Worry seems to be such a fact of life in this society that we have come to the point where we can use its absence as an indicator of what is good.

When I was a psychotherapist, I would hear women (mostly—sometimes men) explore and explore and explore their intimate relationships. After years of listening to people, I began to see patterns in what I was hearing. More and more people described good as the absence of awful: "My husband doesn't drink, he doesn't beat me, and he doesn't run around with other women—I must have a good marriage."

When I would ask these people what they wanted or what would be a good relationship for them, my questions were met with blank stares. They had no clue.

What does it say about the way we have come to think and the way we have come to live when we can define good only as the absence of awful.

Good need not be defined as the absence of awful or terrible. I have inside me the referent point of what is good for me.

Limiting God

My problem is, why would God take an interest in my little problems?

NAN

Maybe we have made our God too small ... the old man in a long white robe with the gray beard (looking a lot like a human being!) or a celestial switchboard with incoming and outgoing calls and Lily Tomlin handling the plugs (looking a lot like a machine) or a confessional booth with a robed figure on the other side handing out penitence and tasks for so many indulgences (a good Catholic version) or Yahweh on the mountain barking out commandments amid thunder and lightning (a good old-fashioned God).

In trying to make God like ourselves we have limited God to our imaginations. As I look around me at this marvelous world and I wonder at the neck of a giraffe, the colors of a butterfly, the ingenuity of a banana slug, I blush to think that I would dare to limit God with my limited imagination.

In limiting God, I limit myself beyond measure.

Being Prepared

Worry is remote preparation.
— ANNE WILSON SCHAEF

It's important to be prepared! Remember Boy Scouts and Girl Scouts? Their motto is "Be Prepared."

How much of our lives have we built upon the belief that if we are just prepared for every possible exigency, we can somehow (magically, perhaps?) keep it from happening? Preparedness, if done properly, can, we hope, be a very effective form of avoidance. Or, if we cannot completely avoid whatever it is that we were sure we needed to avoid, then at least we are ready for it.

We expend a lot of energy on getting ready, especially in our minds. What if this happened? . . . then. The unplanned or the unprepared holds the real terror. Perhaps we could save a lot of time by just trying to deal with what is happening now. No control issues here!

When I spend my time preparing for what might happen, I am missing what is happening.

Control/Living in the Moment

*It's a good thing I worried about it or it would
never have happened that easily.*

CHUCK

Isn't it amazing how far our illusion of control extends
itself? Here we live in a world that is constantly moving
and changing with new possibilities around every corner, and we actually have come to believe that our *worrying* made a store appear just when we needed it or a
task that we had to complete go more smoothly!

We have come to believe in a very simple cause-and-
effect universe. If we do this, then that will happen. If we
don't do this, then we can't keep that from happening. . . .
Better to worry and be on the safe side, regardless.

How much more energy we would have for the
things that present themselves to us in each moment if
we were living in that moment.

*Being in the moment and living each moment make
life easy—worrying each moment into existence makes
life much harder.*

Being Good

It is very hard to be simple enough to be good.
RALPH WALDO EMERSON

That's right! Emerson said it all. Being good is very simple. It may not always be easy and it is very simple. We have heard a lot about doing unto others as we would like to have done unto us, and there's a lot of wisdom in that idea. It's simple: We treat others as we would like to be treated. Yet, it is difficult for modern human beings to let that simple idea alone.

First we need to figure out how we would like to be treated. Now, that's a biggie. As modern thinkers, we can always muck that up with focusing on other people and trying to psych out what they want, how they want it, when they want it, and what might really happen if we did, indeed, give them what they want. Then, we have to build on that and see if we possibly could have what they want, and if we do think we have it, could they take it if we offered it, and, of course, how would we feel if we have gone to all that trouble figuring out all this and they don't even want it . . .

Whew, Emerson was right! It <u>is</u> "hard to be simple enough to be good."

Happiness/Feelings

*I always feel sorry for people who think more
about a rainy day ahead than sunshine today.*

RAE FOLEY

Happiness is right now. How often we rob ourselves of
the happiness we are experiencing in the moment because we are afraid that it will go away. If it goes away,
have we wasted the moment we had to experience it?

Happiness, like many other feelings, is fleeting. It
will come and it will go. That's what feelings do. They
come and go. However, if we refuse to feel them when
they are there, they will always give us problems down
the road.

Our feelings are signposts that give us much needed
information. When we attend to them, listen to them,
and learn from them, they can be very good teachers.
Yet, what they are giving us and what they are teaching
us is right now, not tomorrow.

*So many people destroy relationships by refusing to en-
joy the happiness that is present today and worrying
about what tomorrow will bring.*

Spirituality

*Spirituality is a kind of virgin wisdom, a knowing
that comes prior to experience.*

MARILYN FERGUSON

Can it be possible that we don't have to learn everything the hard way? Is it possible that we can have a "knowing" without having to get our head bloody in the process?

Suppose, just suppose, that our spirituality is something with which we are born. Imagine that we do not have to hunt for it; nor do we have to be taught it. Our spirituality is there because *we* are.

And, because we have it, it is always at our disposal. We can call upon our spiritual selves whenever we need, as often as we need, and that "virgin wisdom" will be available to us throughout our lives. We have but to notice it.

If my spirituality is a given of my existence, then I can operate from a base of perpetual wisdom.

Participation

Don't anticipate with worry . . . participate with joy!

CATHERINE KINEAVY DUGAN

Participation is the only constant invitation that we have from life. This is our life. We have the possibility of living it and participating in it. Of course, if we are going to participate fully in our lives, this robs us of the option of pulling out of our lives and trying to manipulate ourselves and our world. If we are fully participating in our lives, we have very little time and energy to stand back and look . . . and worry!

It is difficult to worry when we are participating fully in anything. Worry requires distraction and when we are distracted, we are not participating.

Also, participating fully is an act of intimacy. We cannot hold back and be intimate, whether it is with another person or with life. Intimacy requires all of us . . . and often, all of us with joy.

Participation and intimacy are intimately connected.

Personality Changes

*Worry changes your personality. People change
when they worry.*

BETTY

Does worry, indeed, change my personality? Once, when
my daughter was about eighteen months old, I came
home from a physical checkup with the information that
I had a "questionable" pap smear and the G.P. wanted
me to make an appointment with my gynecologist for a
follow-up. I immediately phoned my gynecologist and he
agreed to see me first thing the next morning. I was only
twenty-seven or twenty-eight years old and I was frightened and worried. I had very little information from my
family doctor except that he seemed worried and concerned. By the time I arrived home, I had taken on his
feelings.

When I walked through the door, I wanted to withdraw into myself and worry . . . properly. My daughter
could sense the change in me, and instead of her usual
behavior of greeting me and playing with me for a short
time and then going off to play, she kept pecking away
at my wall and trying to get through to me. She had noticed the change in me. I *had* changed. I wasn't the
mother she knew.

**When I change my personality through worry it af-
fects those I love the most.**

Interest/Wonder

Nothing is interesting if you're not interested.
HELEN MACINNESS

What an idea! Interest resides within me! I can have the most beautiful painting or piece of art in the world right in front of my nose and, yet, if I am not interested in it, it is nothing to me.

I can be confronted with magical mind-stretching ideas and if I am not interested, they mean nothing. I will only pursue those things that are of interest to me. And, if I am all bound up in my own problems and my own obsessions about my life and the things I am trying to control in it, I will not be very interested in much of anything.

When we open ourselves to wonder, it is all around us. We have only to become interested to begin to see with different eyes.

Only I can imbue my world with interest and wonder. Only I have the possibility of seeing what is there. Interest is in me . . . not out there.

Growth

I see how I'm addicted to worrying. Last month it
was about this new job. Now that I'm in the job
and enjoying it, I notice my brain go out like a
radar trying to find something else to worry about.

PETE

Sometimes, I think, it's good to have old friends on whom we can depend. Addicts in recovery often say that their "character defects" of control, dishonesty, fear, self-centeredness, and so forth are old friends not so easily given up. If we have grown up in dysfunctional families, these very characteristics that are now killing us may once have been our tools for survival.

It's difficult to see how tools that have served us so well in the past have now become agents of our destruction. And, they have.

There is nothing more frightening than the thought of letting go of old friends, even if they are killing us.

It is important to remember that no one is forcing us to let go of anything. As we do our work, grow, and participate in our lives, we discover a process of moving on.

Growth is a process, not an event, and no one is forcing us to do it.

Laughter

God hath made me to laugh so that all that hear
will laugh with me.

SARAH, GENESIS, THE BIBLE

Laughter is the cleanser of the soul . . . not a scrub brush
that scours and prickles and hurts. Laughter is a gentle
breeze that moves into the crevices of our body and
smoothes the wrinkles out of our insides just as the
wind, without heat, irons out the clothes on the line.

Laughter is the moisturizer that seeps into our
callousness and softens from within what has been
toughened from its rubbing against the world.

Laughter is an infectious disease that can spread
like wildfire, killing nothing but despair.

Laughter is a gift of being human that can be
shared with those we love and those we hate.

How long has it been since you've had a good laugh?

Cultural Training/Control/Perspective

*Worry came in with the White culture and it will
probably go out with it.*

AMERICAN INDIAN ELDER

What an idea! Could it be that worry is culturally
based? Could it be that worry exists only in a culture
that is based upon the illusion of control? Could it be
that worry is not inherent in humanity but is only a creation of our culture that we have been told is reality?

Fortunately, we have the wisdom and perspective
of an Elder from a very ancient culture telling us that
one of our inventions, which we thought and have been
taught was the result of evolution, might be peculiar to
us. Also, that same Elder is telling us that our culture
with its need to worry will not last forever.

Recently, an article in *Time* magazine compared
Western culture to other world cultures that had de-
clined and found an amazing number of similarities.
We can, perhaps, put our lives in perspective if we can
put our culture in perspective and let ourselves see
how many of our struggles are culturally based and not
reality-based.

*I am, of course, a product of my culture. It's comforting
to know that we both can change.*

Imagine away in Forest.
No Expectation
No Goals
Just Being.

Asking for Help

*Nappies on a clothesline are an internationally
recognized distress signal.*

JENNIFER DOROTHY

There is an old African saying, "It takes a whole village
to raise a child." How often in Western culture the task
which requires many to complete successfully is attempted by only one person or at the very most two. An
old Australian Aboriginal Elder once said to me with
great sadness in his eyes and voice, "We think it is very
primitive for a child to have only two parents."

No wonder mothers worry. They are trying to do an
impossible task, raising children alone or, if they are
lucky, with one or two helpers.

It's okay to ask for help. We have been taught that
to need and ask for help is a sign of failure, but better an
imagined failure than a "chins up" disaster.

**The world has not always responded to our "distress
signals," so now may be the time to move to more direct methods of communication.**

Parenting

*I see that my parents were trying to medicate their
own fears and powerlessness at having a child with
a handicap—epilepsy—by worrying.*

JIM

There is nothing more scary, fearful, helpless—or
lonely—than having a child with a disability. Parenting
is not easy under any circumstances and some of us are
given more to cope with than others.

Even if we do not have a physically challenged
child or even if we don't have children, most of us can
identify with trying to find ways of medicating our fears
and feelings of powerlessness.

What if instead of "medicating" our fears and powerlessness we let ourselves feel these feelings without
trying to medicate them with anything.

Fear is a part of living. We all are afraid sometimes.
There's nothing wrong with being afraid. Usually, our
fear of fear is the problem, and not the fear itself. Like-
wise, we often feel powerless because we are! Actually,
we are powerless over much of life. The sooner we realize this powerlessness, the better off we will be. That's
where spirituality begins.

**When I learn to be more inventive about my inventing
I may not have to invent so much.**

Reality

He is as good as his word—and his word is no good.

SEAMUS MACMANUS

One of the messes we set up for ourselves in this life is insisting on trusting people who are not trustworthy. We would very much like the world to be the way we wish it would be. With a little improvement here and there (of course, carefully fitted to our specifications), things would just be so much better.

We would really like it if people *were* as good as their word, and if they are not going to be that way we will force them into it by refusing to see how they really are and *demanding* (ever so politely) that they comply. When they don't (let's face it, this happens quite often), we feel betrayed and furious. Not only have they failed, we have!

One of the greatest forms of wisdom is seeing people as they are, not as we want them to be.

Control

Guidelines from a worry group at Pennsylvania State University:

1. Set up worry period, exclusively for worrying, for thirty minutes every day at the same time.

2. Learn to identify the symptoms of worry—an inability to concentrate, a sinking feeling in the stomach, sweaty palms. Write your worries in a diary so you can review them later. It helps to put a worry out of your mind, at least temporarily.

3. Focus your attention away from your worries—make a phone call, clean your oven, take a walk with a friend.

4. Do not look at your list of worries until the next worry period.

5. When you do look at the list, think your worries through. Try to come up with solutions— worries that are solved are no longer worries.

AS REPORTED BY AMY H. BERGER

Whew! What's wrong with this picture? How we long to have a tight little control fix for our control issues! If worry is an attempt to control our past, our present, and our future, why not try to develop a method to control our need to control. It's logical, isn't it?

Yes, logical—it just doesn't make any sense. It's not surprising that psychology develops approaches based on the illusion of control.

How come it never works when our solution is another form of the problem we are trying to solve?

Negativity/Faith

Fear is faith that it won't work out.
SISTER MARY TRICKY

Fear is like an insurance policy. We pay money to bet that we won't live, and then we do everything we can to win the bet.

It's difficult to see fear as faith and, yet, I think Sister Mary Tricky is right. Our faith becomes confused and misplaced at times.

Our experiences have told us time and time again that things do work out. They may not work out the way we thought they would or the way we thought we wanted them to and . . . they do work out.

One of my mantras in life has become: "This isn't how I thought it would look." I have discovered that this outcome does not necessarily mean that things are *bad*. Often, it only means that I have just been short on imagination.

Negative faith doesn't bring about many positive results.

Food Distractions

*I always worry about food when I go someplace.
"Will I be able to get enough?" "Will I like what
they have to eat?" "Will it be healthy food?"
Sometimes I just give up and take it all with me.*

ANONYMOUS

Food is a universal focus of worry. I'm not talking about situations where people are starving and there really isn't enough food. I am talking about situations where people have more than enough.

When I began to look at the process of worry and the content of worry, I discovered that many people choose food as their favorite worry focus. Will I get what I need? Will I get what I want? Will there be enough?

I often wonder what is going on underneath the focus on food. My guess is that the focus upon food is a distraction for deeper feelings that are even more frightening to face.

When we use food and worry over food as a distraction, we may never have the opportunity to see what's really bugging us.

Anxiety

Our anxiety measures the distance we are from God.

TAYLOR

When I am in touch with my spiritual foundation, anxiety is superfluous. The further away I get from my awareness of the oneness of all things and my knowing that I am an integral part of that oneness, the more anxious I become.

Philosophers have talked about "existential angst." When I try to step out of myself and make myself something to be observed and manipulated, and when I try to step out of all creation and make all of creation something to be observed and manipulated, I become anxious. I have disconnected myself from myself and my grounding.

Many of us have disconnected ourselves from our spiritual base in the service of the god of objectivity, and in so doing have begun the process of distancing ourselves from the ground of our being.

When I am separate from myself and my Creator, I am anxious. Who wouldn't be?

Overtime

When I was forty I had lived over fifty years because I did a lot of overtime.

MYLER MAGRATH

Putting in overtime on life seems a worthless decision. Maybe it's time to stop and take stock and see how many of the things that we do every day are adding to our "overtime" without our even getting paid double time.

Worry is one. How much of our "worry time" could be spent doing something that we want to do or something the person we are worrying about would want us to do? Some of us are good at doing "double time" and can work our worry in while we are doing other things. And, I am not sure that is efficient. We may just be giving part of ourselves to each task.

Control is another unrewarding job. There's not much that we really control in this life. And, if we really can control it, it may not have much life. One thing that is certain about control (or the illusion of control, as I call it) is that it sure can age us fast. Maybe that's where we get to count our overtime.

When I'm doing overtime in life, I'm probably not doing life.

Creative Worry

*When my sister was alive, I worried about her. If
she was okay, I had my Dad to worry about.
When they both died, I shifted to worrying about
my cat. After Blue died, I noticed I started to
worry about the roses I had planted in my back
yard. Now that they are asleep under mounds of
snow, I am worrying about the birds who may not
be finding enough to eat.*

SHEILA

One good thing about worry, it adds a certain comforting
structure to our lives. Also, it's handy and it's flexible.
We can carry it with us wherever we go. It doesn't need
to be kept on ice lest it spoil. The mental space it claims
is rarely matched by physical space requirements and it
travels well.

Worry is flexible in that once we have learned the
basic skills we can attach it to almost anything and it
works equally well. It is a marvelous opportunity to explore vast areas of creativity within ourselves.

It's difficult to imagine anything we could buy that
has as many attributes as worry. We should take more
credit for our imaginative creations.

Nothing is all bad.

Turning Over

Every evening I turn worries over to God. He's going to be up all night anyway.

MARY C. CROWLEY

What a sensible idea! And so practical too! Why should everyone stay awake?

I like the idea of God staying up all night anyway. Now, I wouldn't want to *ask* God to stay up just to handle my worries, but since that seems to be God's S.O.P. (Standard Operating Procedure), I suppose it wouldn't be too much to ask him to take on a few of my problems too—just for the night. We wouldn't want to ask too much. Would we?

Also, there's the business of turning our worries over. Most of the things that we worry about are too big for us anyway or we wouldn't be worrying about them. If we could fix them, we would have done so a long time ago.

Then, why not turn them over to a power greater than ourselves? There must be one somewhere.

It's comforting to think of a twenty-four-hour, seven-day-a-week, on-duty God handling my worry shift for me.

Advice-Giving

Never give cherries to pigs or advice to a fool.

IRISH PROVERB

I don't know much about giving cherries to pigs. What do you suppose happens? Are they too good for pigs? Will pigs get sick? Do they swallow them pits and all? Can they not digest the pits? This whole thing could give me cause for concern.

I do know something about giving advice, though. One of the major things I know is—the only person who is more foolish than the fool who won't accept advice is the fool who is giving it.

When it comes right down to it, the only people we really know anything about and have any hope of changing are ourselves.

We can share our experience with others, we can share our perceptions with others, and we can even share our learnings—and—the rest is up to them. It is when we try to control what they do with this information that we get in trouble.

If I don't want to look like a fool, I need not be one.

Trouble

Worry, the interest paid by those who borrow trouble.

GEORGE WASHINGTON LYON

Life is just one tuition payment after another.

Whenever we look for trouble, we are sure to find it. If it has already happened, we can't change it anyway. If it is happening right now, we'd better just get busy and deal with it and not take the luxury of worrying about it. And, if it *may* happen in the future, we might as well relax, deal with today, and see what happens. This can certainly keep us occupied enough without having to borrow trouble and having to pay interest on it.

The problem is ... some of us just don't have enough to do, so we borrow trouble.

Borrowing trouble debts the present and the future.

Sadness

Take my word for it, the saddest thing under the sky is a soul incapable of sadness.
COUNTESSE CATHERINE DE GASPARIN

How precious is our sadness! The other day I left someone who was very dear to me. We were only to be parted for a short time. Yet, the sadness helped me know the sweetness of the time we had together.

I recently spent some time in Ireland. I love it there. The winding roads, the greenness, my friends, the mists on the hills, and the ferned glens where the fairies still linger and support my being and help my heart soar.

Most of us have places that are sacred to us. These spots, wherever they are, seem to rejuvenate us and lighten our beings. It's not important where the place is. It may be a corner of a room, a place where we like to walk, or a secret place inside ourselves. Wherever it is, when we have taken the time to rest there, even for a bit, we always benefit.

Yet, when our lingering comes to an end, our sadness lets us know how precious the place is to us.

My sadness often exists only to remind me of the joy in my life.

Spare Time

*I'm not one of these people who worries all the
time. I only worry when I have spare time.*

ANONYMOUS

Thank goodness! It's important to know that there are
some people who have a proper perspective on worrying!

Spare time can be a problem. Many of us are terrified if we find ourselves with time on our hands. We
know what to do when we are busy and we certainly
know *how* to keep busy. It's those slow, creeping hours
when we have nothing planned and nothing we *have* to
do that strike terror in our bones.

In fact, many of us seek desperately to fill our days
and nights so we never have to be faced with that specter,
that dread of modern women and men . . . spare time!

Thank goodness we have an ally to help us fend off
the horror of nothing to do. We can always worry.
What a relief!

**No matter how we try to fill our lives, we will, on
occasion, end up with spare time. We might as well
face the dragon right now.**

Road-Making

*Listen Pilgrim! There are no roads. Roads are
made by walking.*

RICHARD ROHR

We often have the illusion that life would be so easy if
we just had well-made modern roads, good road signs,
and a carefully drawn map. Well, that's not the way it
is. Life is a journey, and no one has ever walked our particular path before. We are, indeed, pilgrims. We only
know where the road is going as we walk it and often
then only as we look back to see where we have been.

Though sometimes frightening, this mystery is the
joy and the excitement of life. No one else can take our
journey for us or make our road.

Sometimes we get so terrified that we just want to
stand still, stay put, and not risk the road-making. Yet,
that's what life's really about, isn't it? . . . road-making.

**Spiritual highways are made by pilgrims walking their
individual roads arm in arm.**

Material Worries

I have lost everything, and I am so poor now that
I really cannot afford to let anything worry me.
JOSEPH JEFFERSON

I wonder how much of our worrying is tied up with our material world. In a world with a science that teaches us to value only what can be registered with our senses or extensions of our senses, we have come to believe that wealth truly lies in our material possessions. We have labored under the illusion that if we just had enough money and things, we would never have to worry again. Yet, is worry a luxury? Is worry related to a wealth of things and a poverty of the soul? I wonder.

If we cannot afford to let anything worry us, are we not rich? So many of our children's stories teach us that wealth is not in things but in the untouchable, the unstorable, the uncollectable. The mystery of life lies not in what we can grasp; it is in the fleeting, the almost felt and the almost known.

Can any of us really afford to worry? Maybe not being able to afford letting anything worry us will help us shift our focus.

Minding Our Own Business

The idea of strictly minding our own business is
moldy rubbish. Who could be so selfish?

MYRTLE BARKER

Agreed! Where would we be if we all just minded our own business? What would we do with our time? We can hardly imagine that we actually have enough business to keep us occupied anyway. Besides, there are plenty of people out there who need our expert advice, our wisdom, and our experience. Keeping all this valuable stuff to ourselves would be selfish indeed!

If we did start minding our own business we might find that our lives are not defined by others. They are defined by what we do with them. We might even find that this is true for others, too.

If we started minding our own business, we might discover that it is interesting, and we might even grow and expand.

If we started minding our own business, we might discover that no one else can handle it better than we can, and this might be true for others, too.

Yet, none of us wants to be selfish. Do we?

Security

*Today is the tomorrow you worried about
yesterday.*

JERRY LONGAN

And you know what? Tomorrow will be the same thing!

I guess there's a certain comfort in sameness. We go to great lengths to give ourselves the illusion of security. If we just had enough . . . money, property, things, love, happiness, insurance policies, financial plans, power, organizational plans . . . whatever. If we just had enough we would be all right.

Where did we get this illusion of security? How much of our lives is focused upon this illusion?

Can we really delude ourselves into believing that we can make static a moving universe, a universe in process?

Instead of trying to achieve such highly developed skills in making our lives static, we could, instead, learn to live with a life and a world in process.

When we are in process with our universe, there's not much to worry about. And even if there is, it can be done tomorrow.

Pain/Creativity

*We satisfied ourselves the other day that there was
no real ill in life except severe bodily pain;
everything else is the child of the imagination, and
depends on our thoughts. All other ills find a
remedy either from time, or moderation, or
strength of mind.*

LA MARQUISE DE SIVIGNE

Funny thing about severe physical pain: when we are
experiencing it, we don't have the time or the energy to
worry about it. We just have to focus all our energy on
coping with it. It is an interesting idea that this kind of
pain is really the only ill in life and that everything else
is a child of our imagination.

Our imaginations are so active. Our brains are so
creative, such masters at the "what might be." When we
are in the "what might be," we are never in the "is."

What a beautiful thought, that all other ills can be
healed by "time, moderation, or strength of mind." I
would probably substitute faith for strength of mind, but
who cares? The important thing is to take a look at how
many of our troubles are creations of our own mind.

The beauty here is . . . if I created it, I can uncreate it.

Holy Relationships

If I worry enough, it is a plea to God that it won't happen.

TIFFANY

What a strange form of prayer! I can just see God up there getting bombarded with worries and trying to figure out that they are really prayers. This prayer is a strange mixture of control and indirect communication. Tricky but not unusual.

We often believe that we can control our lives and the future by worrying and we add to it our belief that we can control God. What a hoot!

Then, instead of a personal, straightforward talk with God, being honest about what we want and don't want, we muck around and try to set it up so that we can subtly get what we want without having to be direct. Does this, I wonder, have any resemblance to the way we try to do our relationships with the people around us? Probably not, but we might want to take a look at it.

Then, after all that good communication about what we really want, are we ready to let it go and leave it up to a power greater than ourselves? (I doubt it.)

Isn't it strange how we try to use techniques on God that haven't worked with our family and friends?

Expectations/Anticipation

The misfortunes hardest to bear are these which never came.

JAMES RUSSELL LOWELL

We worriers can do a lot with "what if's." How many times have we carefully worked out what we thought would happen, how we would respond, and how the other person would respond, only to find that all of our assumptions and expectations had completely missed the mark and we were prepared for something that never happened?

How much time we waste in what might have been when we have only to deal with what is! Often the anticipation is much worse than dealing with the actual event, no matter how horrible it is. Pain is that way. I think we cause pain by anticipating it. Better to deal with it as we must.

Nothing in the Constitution says I have to torture myself before the event.

Planning

*Planning ahead . . . in business it's called a
budget, in the middle of the night it's called* WORRY.
BETSY MARTIN

We have consistently been told that we have to PLAN.
We need to look ahead and be able to see where we are
going or want to go. In fact, the best planners are thought
to be those who can predict accurately and then control.
Consultants are paid dearly to tease out every possible
contingency and then plan for it, leaving nothing to
chance . . . or so we think.

If we have bought into this model, it's no wonder
we have become a society of worriers.

Actually, there's nothing wrong with planning.
Planning can be fun and we can play with all kinds of
possibilities in our heads and in our hearts. The trouble
comes with what we *do* with it. Last summer, I had
planned to take long walks, ride horseback, exercise,
and renew my skating. I had great fun thinking about it
and was really looking forward to the summer. Then, I
had a machete accident and almost had my foot severed
at the ankle. I spent the summer in a cast, "retraining"
my foot to walk . . . not what I had planned. Yet, I had a
good summer.

*Plans are okay. It's only when we try to make them
happen, use them to miss other opportunities, and
refuse to let them go that we get into trouble.*

Relationships

When I am worrying about whether a relationship will last or not, I have already left it.

ANNE WILSON SCHAEF

Relationships are a favorite focus for worriers. Sometimes, I think we believe that we can actually worry a relationship into existence. Often, once we have started a relationship, we act as if one of the ways to keep it alive is to worry it all the time and never give it a rest. I have to admit, this does add to the excitement and the adrenaline. I doubt that, ultimately, it enhances the relationship. How difficult it is to just let a relationship be, not manage or direct it, and just participate in it.

It is often difficult to see that when we are worrying about whether the relationship will last or not, we are not nurturing the relationship. The very fact of worrying about it means that we have stepped out of it emotionally, mentally, and probably spiritually, and have begun to observe it from outside. This is a sure killer.

Relationships are meant to be participated in, not observed.

Spirituality

Between God and me, there is no "between."
MEISTER ECKHART

"Between" implies separation and sides. I have had the experience of people perceiving a struggle between me and another person and then saying, "I don't want to get in between you two; I don't want to take sides." It is peculiar that differences of opinion always seem to imply two opposite sides.

Modern psychology has taught us that if two people are having a conflict, both people must be responsible. In recovery circles, however, I have learned that one person can be clear and the other "in their addictive disease" when differences arise, and then there are no "sides." One can be clear while the other is involved in "stinkin' thinkin'." In our society of dualisms, we have come to think in terms of choosing between this and that.

But, why put spirituality in a dualistic realm? It doesn't fit. When I am one with God, I am one with myself. When I am one with myself, I am one with God. When I am both one with myself and with God, I am one with all life and all the processes of life, and "between" has no meaning.

"Between" probably has no place in true oneness.

Saying the Right Thing/Arrogance

Julie worries about what she says to people. After school, she returns home to recount the day's conversations to her mother, husband, and children, asking them, "So what do you think?"

QUOTED BY AMY H. BERGER

How arrogant we have become when we truly believe that we can control how other people respond to what we say! How many research skills of the highest order have we developed to collect data on our conversations? We try to learn how to say things exactly the right way in order to bring about the desired effect (some "mistakenly" call this manipulation). We try to anticipate what the other person will say so we have a proper response. And, then we have computerlike memories of what they said and what we said, when we/they said it, and how we/they sounded so we can "process" it with others. Whew. What a lot of work! . . . And . . . then we worry about the entire conversation.

It's important not to blurt out everything that comes to our minds, especially if we aren't clear. And, it's important to take responsibility for what we say. Yet, ultimately, when we really come down to it, the best we can do with anything is make our mistakes and learn from them.

Getting it "right" may not be as important as getting it.

Laughter

*Laughing stirs up the blood, expands the chest,
electrifies the nerves, clears away the cobwebs
from the brain, and gives the whole system a
cleansing rehabilitation.*

ANONYMOUS

How silly of me ... I just thought laughter was great fun!

Have you ever had a giggle attack? You know, one of those times when you and usually a friend or two start laughing and you just can't stop? You are sure that you are going to wet your pants, the tears are rolling down your cheeks, your brain is saying, "Honestly! this isn't very dignified," your gut feels like an overinflated tire that will soon burst, you feel completely at the will of the giggle, and whenever you look up and catch eyes with your friends, you start all over again? The experience is much like being tumbled in a rough surf with not a prayer of getting your feet solidly on the sand. You know what I mean?

Isn't it great to know that the giggle experience is good for the body?!

My body needs laughter just as it needs tears. Both are cleansers.

Control/Wisdom

Me hirau atu te ra koia, i haramia ra?

Can I pull the sun down with a forked stick, or prevent it from running its course?

MAORI PROVERB

One of the blessings I have received in the last several years is the opportunity to be invited to sit with Native people and their Elders throughout the world. In so doing, I have not only been able to listen to their wisdom as they spoke, I have had access to the proverbs of their culture. I have developed a special fondness for proverbs, an awareness of similarities from culture to culture and an appreciation for the wisdom hidden in them. We need wisdom in our lives . . . from as many sources as possible.

What better way to confront the absurdity of the illusion of control than in a proverb? It does seem a little silly, doesn't it, when we think about attempting to prevent the sun from running its full course by pulling it down with a forked stick. Most of our attempts at control fall into the same general category: silliness.

Wisdom is wisdom
Whether old or new
It is fitting for everyone
For me and for you

Trust

I have been familiar with the process of worry for
a long time; as I learn to trust my Higher Power
more, worry becomes less . . . worrisome.

JIM

Some say that worry is a fault in trust. It is difficult to trust a power greater than ourselves when we have been taught that there is no such thing (except maybe money) and even if there is, it (she/he) has really made a mess of things. Besides, we come from a land of rugged individualism. We are supposed to be able to take care of our families, our businesses, and ourselves alone. No wonder we worry. Faced with an impossible mandate, one sensible response is to worry.

For most of us, it's not possible to switch on "trust" at a moment's notice, especially after the strict training to be "in charge." It takes time to figure out the gauntlets to put a Higher Power through before we are sure it (she/he) can be trusted and to check and recheck our data to make sure that it is valid and we haven't been fooled somewhere along the line.

After all, one of the things we can worry about is whether a Higher Power can really be trusted.

Lies

The gods could not be honored by lies.

THEANO

"The gods could not be honored by lies" and neither can we. Yet, lying has become so ingrained in the warp and woof of our culture that we often do not even know when we are lying.

Do we fake orgasm or sexual enjoyment, do we use headaches or tiredness to avoid intimacy when we know that neither is the issue, are we nice when we're homicidal, or at least furious with a person, or do we dress in a way that is not comfortable for us because it's the accepted costume in certain circles? What about those subtle little things? Do we let people walk away with a false impression because it is easier, do we deliberately mislead and let the other person take the responsibility for the misunderstanding, do we complain about the food in the restaurant and then when the waiter asks, "How is your meal?" we say, "Fine"?

Every little lie erodes our soul—even if we get away with it.

Responsibility

Worry is not a choice. It is an obligation.
ANNE WILSON SCHAEF

For those of us who are true believers in worry and who are accomplished worriers, worry does not seem like a choice. In fact, to think of worry as a choice seems absurd. Worry is something we do. It's not that we like to worry (well, maybe a little!), we simply have no choice.

Also, we believe that worry is a responsibility and an obligation. How will people know we love them if we don't worry about them? How can we possibly be conscientious or concerned people if we don't worry about the world and what's happening? If people don't do their share of worrying, will the world just fly into a million little pieces? Maybe worry is like prayer. If enough people do it the world can continue revolving on its axis.

When we practice our obsessions, that is not concern, that is obsession.

Beliefs

The passing of any belief is never a happy event for those that hold it.

DEANE JUHAN

One of the confusions each of us has to wrestle with daily is the distinction between a belief and a fact. We have been trained to believe that facts are ideas that have been "proven" by modern science and backed up with numbers. We all know that statistics lie and most statistics are based on probabilities that may or may not apply to any specific case. Yet, we choose to ignore what we know in our hearts, for we have come to believe in what modern science has taught us. Science has *become* our belief system.

When we get right down to it, there are very few real "facts" in this world. Our fragile spider web of existence is held together by gossamer threads of beliefs we hold near and dear. Yet, like a huge celestial spider web, these fine threads can completely immobilize us if we begin to give them substance and come to believe that they are solid.

An old African proverb says, "A spider web can hold a lion." It's up to us to see that our beliefs do not become prison bars.

Aloneness/Isolation

I worry the most when I'm alone.

BETTY

What a loss it is that we have come to think that when no one else is around we are with no one. When we are alone we are, indeed, with one of the most important people in our lives. If we use our alone-time to worry, we transform alone-time into isolation, and isolation will destroy us.

With alone-time, we have the possibility of creativity, serenity, experiencing our spirituality, resting, and healing.

Isolation brings struggle, pain, feelings of abandonment, fear, and hopelessness. We can choose what we do with our alone-time. When we are tempted to use it in ways that are destructive to ourselves or others we can pray ... call someone ... do something else. We always have choices. When we believe we don't have choices, the only person we are conning is ourself.

When we use our alone-time for worry, we have transformed it into isolation.

Aliveness

Every day's a kick!

OPRAH WINFREY

I am sure that what Oprah says is true. Each day may be a jolly good time, a kick in the butt, or just full. And, one of the things we can be confident about is that every day will be something . . . usually something we have not quite figured out yet.

If we are to live each new day, perhaps our energies are best spent approaching it openly with anticipation and not with expectations. Expectations kill our aliveness and close around us like extra padding that looks soft and cozy but transforms into a suit of armor that lets nothing out or nothing in. Actually, it's probably even impossible to feel a much-needed kick in the pants in a heavy suit of armor.

When we begin to let ourselves have fun with life, it begins to play with us.

Letting Go

But now I am able to say to myself, "I know God is quite capable of doing any worrying necessary around this. I will leave it to God and trust that all is right with the plan."

PAUL

Could it be that God is a better worrier than we are? I doubt it. Worrying seems like a peculiarly human characteristic. Worrying seems to be entirely related to thinking . . . not just any kind of thinking . . . it seems to be related to circular, obsessive thinking. Frankly, it's hard to imagine God indulging in worry. Yet, again, when I think of it, it's hard to imagine just what God does. But, what God does hardly seems to be our problem now, does it?

What is important to our living here is that God, the Creator, the process of the universe, probably has a lot more information than we do on just about everything and if we can just have faith in that process, we can probably relax some.

It's very difficult for worriers to do their legwork in life and then . . . just let it go. Sounds like heresy, doesn't it?

Possibilities

*All things are possible until they are proved
impossible—even the impossible may only be so,
as of now.*

PEARL S. BUCK

As worriers, we want to know exactly what's possible
and what's impossible and then go from there. We
would much rather know something is impossible before
we attempt it than attempt it and thus prove it is impossible. This is even worse if we are not really proving that
it's impossible . . . we are only proving that it is impossible for *us* at *that* time in *that* way. I mean really, what's
a good worrier to do? How can we get a firm grasp on
anything? And, if we can't get a firm grasp on anything,
we'd better worry about it. How much of life really is
making the impossible possible?

**When I am worrying about something, I am probably
not trying to do it. When I am trying to do it, I probably don't have time to worry about it. Funny, that!**

Worry as a Referent

Within the space of twenty minutes I noticed saying "I don't have to worry" or "We don't have to worry about that" about three times.

CONNIE

For so many of us, worry has become such an integral part of our lives that we have developed worry as our point of reference. We sort our lives into carefully labeled boxes: things we *definitely* need to worry about; things we *may* need to worry about (they are kept warm just in case); things we *already* have worried about and it didn't do any good; things we worried about where there was a definite payoff (we must keep this in mind!); things we are worried about worrying about; things (a very few, possibly) that we definitely do not need to worry about. (This last one is a tricky category and one we must keep a close eye on, as it could change any moment. Any good, competent worrier knows that!)

When one references one's life to worry, what else is there?

Certainty of Process

*The really frightening thing about middle age is the
knowledge that you'll grow out of it.*

DORIS DAY

What a life this is! We so want the luxury of certainty
in our lives and we quietly (and sometimes not so quietly) go about trying to arrange our lives to guarantee it.
Then, when we have it, we don't think it's such a good
thing. Ah, such is the fate of the human organism.

So often we forget that life is a process and that we
as people are a process. We are not immutable objects,
although we and others may treat us as such. We are
continually unfolding. We truly cannot stop that
process. We can sidetrack it, we can block it, we can try
to put it off, we can try to push it, we can even try to ignore it and deny it and, whatever we do, the process
continues.

One of the things that we rarely think to do with
our life process is to participate in it . . . nothing big . . .
nothing complex . . . just participate with it.

**When a riptide catches us, if we ride it, it will usually
take us out to sea and then dump us on shore somewhere else. If we fight it, we die.**

Sharing

Insanity: When I worry about your worrying
about what I tell you I'm worrying about.
So I worry alone rather than get support.

JUNE

One of the ways we worriers have learned to cope is by not telling others about our worrying for fear they will start worrying. Somehow, we believe we are such good cons that if we don't tell others about our worrying they will not know that we are worrying. It is a peculiar form of arrogance and self-centeredness to believe that we are so good at disguising our worry that others will not notice. The other side of the coin of self-centeredness is to labor under the illusion that our moods do not affect those nearest to us or that we can hide them from those who love us the most.

Often, sharing our concerns gives us an opportunity to let them go. We do need to look carefully, however, at whether we are really ready to give them up. If we're not, nothing will work.

Remember, those who genuinely care about us truly want to know what's going on with us.

Action

You'll never plow a field by turning it over in your mind.

IRISH PROVERB

How important action is in our lives! In the time it takes to get caught in circular, obsessive thinking, we could be helping someone else.

How often have we become enmeshed in the downward-spiraling process of our own minds until we are so far gone, we feel that no one or nothing can pull us out of it? However, most of us have some clues. We have engaged in this downward spiral often enough that we can recognize the signs ... we begin to think the same thoughts over and over, believing that if we just examine them once again, a solution will present itself ... we begin to pull into ourselves and isolate so we can have more time and energy for our mind games ... we get depressed. When we first recognize the signs of obsessive thinking, it is time to get up and do something for someone else.

Only I can move me to action.

Thinking

You are today where your thoughts have brought you; you will be tomorrow where your thoughts take you.

JAMES ALLEN

Rarely do we realize that our thoughts are just that . . . our thoughts. Because we think them, we often fail to see that they are not necessarily reality. They are our view of reality at that moment . . . nothing less . . . nothing more. Then, if we take the original thought and embellish it, elaborate on it, and build on it, we begin to construct a house of cards which we can move into and start decorating.

Often, our minds are our worst enemies. Or, we let them be. With little effort at all we can think ourselves into a complete tizzy. We cannot actually live in the future . . . but . . . our minds can and do.

It's important to remember that our thoughts aren't real. They are processes that we can observe, find interesting, and then, let go of if we wish.

We can think ourselves in or out of anything. It's the living that's important.

Control/Will

A request not to worry . . . is perhaps the least-
soothing message capable of human utterance.

MIGNON G. EBERHART

Every worrier knows that there are many times when the process of worrying has a life of its own. In fact, being told not to worry may be just the trigger needed to start a small snowball which, as it rolls down the hill, gains in size and momentum.

What if we think of worry as similar to an addictive process? Once the worrying process starts, we are powerless over it. No doubt about that. It truly does make our life unmanageable once we are into it.

Do we believe that there is a power greater than ourselves and that that power can restore us to sanity? Check it out. If so, then we can make a decision to turn our will and our lives over to that power . . . and see what happens. It has worked for millions of people.

Sometimes my will isn't the tool I need.

Letting Go/Reality

What others think about me is none of my business.

ANONYMOUS

So often our worries are centered around what other people think of us or what they might say about us. Much of our time and energy is spent in arranging our lives so that the attention we do get will be approval.

A few years ago, I was involved in a rather nasty court case. I was pained and initially shocked and devastated with the accusations thrown at me and the picture that was being painted of me by the opposing legal team. I knew what the truth was from my perspective and I was appalled by the painful distortions. I found myself obsessing over these distortions and wanting to broadcast the truth to the world. Then, I realized that the people who knew and loved me knew the truth and to the others it probably didn't matter much. Also, that those who were willing to take the bait probably wouldn't work out as friends anyway.

During that difficult time, I rediscovered the saying, "What others think about me and say about me(!) is none of my business," and this saying became my mantra. I learned a new level of letting go of my illusion of control and it was a great gift.

Worrying about things over which we have no control is like spitting into the wind. It only comes back in our faces.

Illusions

*This day is all I have to work with, and it is all I
need. If I am tempted to worry about tomorrow's
concerns, I will gently bring my mind back to the
present*

THE COURAGE TO CHANGE

These are words from an excellent meditation book,
which we may want to ponder. It is difficult sometimes
to realize that this moment is all we have. We hear of
friends being hit by a car or other young healthy people
being struck down in the prime of life, and somewhere
deep in our brains we know that there is no certainty.
Yet, we try to live our lives as if there is.

Rarely do we stop to realize that living our lives
based upon something we know is not true is living an
illusion. It's very hard to keep an illusion alive. We can
spend a great deal of time and effort on this illusion-
maintenance project and, in the end, we are standing
on very shaky ground.

**Maybe, when we realize that we're involved in build-
ing and maintaining illusions that rest on shaky
ground, we'll discover that we have other options.**

Change

I just got tired of worrying . . . so I quit.

PATTI

Sometimes things happen like this. We get a blinding flash of reality and . . . we change.

One of the most marvelous characteristics of the human species is that we can change. We can change slowly over a period of time. Or we can get a flash, like Patti did, and change in an instant.

What a marvelous opportunity change gives us! We always have the possibility of responding differently next time. We have the possibility of new possibilities. We can always develop new skills for new opportunities.

Now, if you're a person who thinks you're going to get everything in order so it will stay that way for the rest of your life, this change stuff could be a problem . . . but only if you make it one.

If change is the given in my life, I will be given a lot.

Indulging

*You can't start worrying about what's going to
happen. You can get spastic enough worrying
about what's happening now.*

                    LAUREN BACALL

Indulging is so indulgent. Sometimes we can see our
plunge into indulging and sometimes we can't. Often
we do not know that we have made the choice to indulge ourselves until we are in the thick of it, and when
we are spinning around in our confusion, the path to
sanity may seem a long way off.

   We need friends around who can notice the signs
of slippage. We need to learn to recognize our own danger signs.

**Once we have committed not to indulge ourselves,
help is only a phone call away.**

Knowing God

You prove but too clearly, that seeking to know is
too frequently learning to doubt.

ANTOINETTE DESHOULIEIES

Isn't this an interesting statement? When we are trying to know something that isn't ready to be known or we are not ready to know, we do begin to doubt. Once we begin to doubt we then attempt to prove or disprove our doubts and before we know it, we are caught up in the muck and mire of our own thoughts.

When I first read this statement, I thought about theology. I have studied theology so I speak from experience. Theology is basically thinking about God. It is an attempt to know God through our minds.

Most of us as children, I believe, know God. Our spirituality is something that is everyday and is integrated into the wholeness of our being. It is only when we begin thinking about God that we become separate.

Maybe this learning to doubt is why Jesus said that we need to become like little children.

Money

*There is nothing so degrading as the constant
anxiety about one's means of livelihood. . . .
Money is like a sixth sense without which you
cannot make a complete use of the other five.*
WILLIAM SOMERSET MAUGHAM

Sometimes we forget that money isn't real. It becomes so concrete and has so much power that we begin to think of it as real and that it has real value.

I remember a few years ago when the value of the American dollar was fluctuating wildly on the world monetary market and so many Americans had their entire world turned topsy-turvy because they believed the dollar was real and absolute.

When I was married, I discovered that my husband and I had very different relationships with money. He was uneasy with money, worried about it, and by self-admission, did not handle it well. I, on the other hand, have a certain ease with money, do well with it, spend it when I have it, save it, and can do well without it. We discovered that our money went further when I handled it. We could sit down with the same amount of money to pay the same amount of bills and I would have more than enough and he would not have enough. Money stretches. It is not real. It is relative.

Money may control the rich far more than it controls the poor.

Crisis

I stopped listening to the radio in the morning. It was so much crisis stuff it affected my day. Why do I want that kind of anxiety? I used it to keep the noise going.

MIA

There is nothing like a good crisis to keep us going. Some of us are better at stirring up a crisis than others and, let's admit it, most of us have at least some skill in this area. Even if we are a little underdeveloped in the area of creating crisis, there is always someone or something, like the media for instance, around to help us. Crisis is the order of the day.

As individuals, and as a society, we have become dependent upon the stimulation of a constant crisis. Notice how many of the bestselling novels and blockbuster movies present us with one crisis after another.

We can get to the point where our lives seem pretty dull without a crisis. Crisis has become the "white noise" in our lives that masks the gentle whisperings of feelings that stir our souls.

How can I possibly be interested in spirituality unless it is accompanied by lightning, thunder, and a celestial orchestra?

Escape from Intimacy

One may worry about a loved one who looks ill or upset or tired.

BETSY MARTIN

Yes, how often do we show our love by worrying? We believe if we really care about someone, we, of course, will worry about them. Worry is a safe and acceptable (!) way of sharing love. The good thing about "love through worry" is that we don't have to get too close. When we worry about someone we love, we don't have to struggle with the discomfort of intimacy. Worrying pulls us into ourselves and away from the other person and we can hide behind walls of concern. Unfortunately, walls of concern are still walls, and walls always separate us from those we love the most.

Worry by its very essence is a self-absorbed activity. When we are worrying, we are not available to anyone, even ourselves.

Becoming unavailable is a good escape from intimacy and it gets confusing when we do it to show love.

Happiness

Whether happiness may come or not one should try and prepare one's self to do without it.

GEORGE ELIOT

Can one ever really prepare to do without happiness and live a full life? I doubt it.

Happiness, like most of the things that happen to us in life, is a gift. We can't make happiness happen. We can, however, keep it from happening. In fact, I suspect that one good way of keeping it from happening is to prepare ourselves to do without it. After all, once we have put all that time into such careful preparation, it would be disappointing to worry and have happiness descend upon us like sunshine on our storm cloud.

Fortunately, life does not usually ask us what we have prepared for and then give it to us. Life is more like the seasoning in a good soup . . . a little of this, a dash of that, a dollop of that over there, and a pinch of something else thrown in for good measure. In the end, it's the whole mixture that makes the soup.

Happiness may be more like the salt than the potatoes in a good vegetable soup.

Humor

"Life is too short for worrying."
"Yes, that's what worries me."

ANONYMOUS

It's about time we laughed a little bit about worry. After all, we worriers are a funny lot. Worrying is the one skill that can be applied to everything in life. Rarely have we developed anything so useful.

We complain about our worrying, but let someone say something bad about worrying or try to take it away from us and we are ready to challenge Goliath himself. We may complain about it and we sure don't want anyone else to. After all, some things are still sacred.

And, remember the times that we thought we could give up worrying whenever we wanted to? We just haven't been ready yet and, besides, it doesn't really harm anyone. Strange. I've heard the same thing about drinking. And you better not tease us about it, either.

When we get humorless about something, we'd better check it out.

Contracts

ARTICLE I

The undersigned transfers to God all worries and problems and God agrees to take over everything that makes her/him frightened, angry, anxious, or unhappy and God is obliged to settle these problems in the best possible manner.

Therewith, the undersigned has transferred her/his worries and problems and has to observe the following:

1. She/he has to list the ten most important worries and problems in the order of importance and has to add this list as an addendum to this contract.

2. Only when a worry has been disposed of and checked off as being settled can a new problem be subsequently subscribed to the responsibility of God.

3. For every resolved problem the undersigned is obliged and agrees to do the following:

a) to give at least three minutes of thanks for God's help.

b) to enjoy the resolution and to look glad.

c) to do something cheerful or to give joy by doing some good deed.

ARTICLE II

The submitted worries transferred according to Article I belong entirely to God. Hence God has the following rights:

God has the agreed right to:

1. Determine the order of the settlement of the worries.

2. Choose the method, procedure, and the speed of the settlement of said worries unconditionally and by himself/herself (itself).

3. Determine to what percentage the undersigned shall be involved in the solution of the problem.

ARTICLE III

God takes the transferred worries very seriously and will not agree to any interference in the settlement. Any breach of contract must be carefully avoided. The following behavior will be deemed a breach of contract:

1. Thinking of certain worries for more than five minutes.

2. Suffering, being angry, and not being able to fall asleep because of worries.

3. Worrying anxiously and being mentally alarmed and tense.

4. Indulging in negative thoughts, looking for something bad in others, complaining, and being unhappy.

5. Returning evil for evil.

6. Feeling insulted, discounted, or humiliated, or by suffering or feeling self-pity.

In case of breach of contract, the undersigned accepts the following obligations:

1. Doing something good for one who suffers.

2. Reading conscientiously pages 85–88 in the *Big Book of Alcoholics Anonymous*.

3. Searching all passages about worries in the book *As Bill Sees It*.

4. Reading the six articles of Bill.

ARTICLE IV

Any worries thus assigned and taken over by God are exclusively God's. The undersigned is not entitled secretly or in public to elicit even a single worry or to deal with it again. She/he may only talk or think about it by being gratefully happy about the above settlement and the additional unsolicited love felt from God.

ARTICLE V

If there are no important worries, the undersigned agrees not to bother God with unnecessary problems and will enjoy life.

ARTICLE VI

The undersigned agrees to take this contract seriously.

_____   _____
Date   *Signature*

EXCERPTED FROM A CONTRACT USED BY THE VIENNA AL-ANON GROUP, TRANSLATED BY JOCUM AND HANS

Well, what do you think? It's a lot better than some contracts I know.

Children/Parenting/Trust

God has no grandchildren.

PROVERB

When I first heard this saying, "God has no grand-children," I knew it had great meaning for me. Yet, I could not quite understand what it was. I had long been comfortable with the idea that everyone (even my children!) has his own Higher Power. I knew that! This proverb was wisely given to me at a time when one of my children was having quite a struggle with his life, and, therefore, I, too, was having quite a struggle with his life. I had accepted that he had his own Higher Power and his own personal and spiritual path . . . or so I thought!

Then I got it! I was willing to admit that he had his own Higher Power *and*, I was sure his was not as experienced as mine (after all, I'm older), did not have the wisdom mine did (my Higher Power did, after all, have the added benefit of *my* wisdom), was possibly not on duty twenty-four hours a day, seven days a week (mine had, after all, learned that full-time duty was essential), and, in general, was just more of a piker than *my* Higher Power. The bottom line was that, just to be sure that things would turn out as they "should," I had to be on duty worrying all the time—with the help of my Higher Power, of course.

WHEW! Thank goodness the relationship with our Creator is not a lineage. Everyone has a direct pipeline!

When I know that "God has no grandchildren," my life gets easier.

Intimacy

*Having someone in the family or other group who
worries relieves other members of the "need" to
worry about things!*

BETSY MARTIN

Many of us have come to believe that there is a "worry
quota" that must be filled. It is such a relief if we have a
spouse or a friend who is willing to pitch in and help us
fill our worry quota. Filling our worry quota by ourselves
is lonely indeed.

Perhaps the issue is not one of trying to find someone to share the worry. Perhaps the issue is taking a
look at our loneliness and the way we approach intimacy. We can never really get close through sharing
worry or through worry itself. In fact, both may be es-
capes from intimacy.

It's important to have someone in our lives with
whom we can share our concerns. Taking the further
step and asking them to be a worry partner is probably a
step away from intimacy, not a step toward it.

**Intimacy is best served when we share a concern and
then take action together.**

Honesty Skills

Honesty without compassion is brutality.

ANONYMOUS

We really know so little about honesty when it comes right down to it. Honesty is certainly not something that is rewarded in our society. Some years ago, I remember someone handing me a translation of a poem by a Russian poet. The basic theme was—what has happened to a society when one person who tells the truth is regarded as courageous? I was very touched by that poem and have become increasingly aware of how unusual honesty is in our daily lives.

Because honesty is so rare, we have few skills for healthy honesty. During the sixties, when the human potential movement introduced an "honesty jag," many people thought honesty meant telling the other person what was wrong with him/her. Wrong!

For honesty to be helpful we need to remember several things: 1) Honesty is most useful when it is a statement about ourselves: "I feel uncomfortable with that." "I don't like that." "That's not acceptable to me." 2) Honesty is helpful when we have a contract for honesty with others. I find that this contract is necessary for me with the people with whom I want to be close. 3) Honesty can be useful when put in the form of noticings (not interpretations): "I notice you flushed when you said that" . . . *and let it go.* 4) Honesty is best used with compassion and caring. If there is any judgmentalism attached, *don't say it.* Get yourself clear first.

We need training in honesty skills.

Self-Centeredness

I see my self-centeredness in worrying about my job, which starts next week—I mean, what makes me think I can't worry about it then?

PETE

It's difficult to see our worry as self-centered even when we are worrying about ourselves. Since much worry can go under the guise of worrying about others, we get away with it. Yet, let's take a look at the possibility of self-centeredness.

First of all, a great deal of worry is *pre*-worry. We are worrying about something that may or may not happen. When we are mentally and emotionally preparing for something that might happen, we withdraw into ourselves and become self-absorbed. Sounds like self-centeredness to me!

When we are worrying about something that *might* happen, we are not trusting that we simply do not have all the wisdom and information about this particular issue and ultimately things will work out as they will, whether it is what we thought we wanted or not. Sounds like self-centeredness to me.

Our self-centeredness is a many-faceted jewel, slowly turning in the sunlight. We have all our lives to discover new facets.

Getting It "Together"

I am not afraid of storms for I am learning how to sail my ship.

LOUISA MAY ALCOTT

Yesterday I tried to call my son in Japan. When the operator and I rang his apartment, we heard a recording that made no sense. Then when she attempted to get the Japanese international operator, she rang and rang and there was no answer. Having dealt with the after-effects of a hurricane in Hawaii two years ago, I said, "Has there been an earthquake or something?" She then swung into action, checked all her information, said there had been, and tried to find out all she could for me.

When I got off the phone, I stretched out and had a good cry. While I was crying a thought went through my head—"I don't need this. I just about have my entire life worked out and everything is going smoothly. Why did this happen? Suppose my son is dead!"—Then I had to laugh. These things that happen don't interfere with my life . . . they *are* my life. This is what life is . . . the things that happen . . . from day to day, week to week, year to year. There will always be storms, we have only to sail our ships.

One nice thing about life is that we will never quite "get it all together." At least, not for long.

Hope/Positivism

*Life is atrocious, we know. But precisely because
I expect little of the human condition, man's
periods of felicity, his partial progress, his efforts to
begin over again and continue, all seem to me like
so many prodigies which nearly compensate for the
monstrous mass of ills and defeats, of indifference
and error. Catastrophe and ruin will come;
disorder will triumph, but order will too, from
time to time.*

MARGUERITE YOURCENAR

We find it so easy to focus on the negative, and certainly there is more adrenaline in the negative, yet, if we just stop for a moment, there is so much good in life.

Not long ago, I was traveling in Germany and I broke a fingernail at the airport. Now, I hate to run around with a jagged, rough fingernail. It catches on everything. I, of course, had packed my manicure set in the bag I checked to make my purse lighter. In poor German, I tried several duty-free shops, looking for a fingernail file. When my last resort said she didn't have one, a woman standing in line said, "Here, take this one. I have two in my purse," and handed me a lovely diamond file. "Are you sure?" I said. "I can use it and give it back." "Very sure," she said. "Someone will do the same for me someday."

Good things happen every day. We have only to notice.

Feelings

Archie doesn't know how to worry without getting upset.

EDITH BUNKER, ON THE TV SHOW
"ALL IN THE FAMILY"

What we really need is a way to learn how to worry without getting upset. After all, it's not really the worrying that is the problem, is it? The real problem is that we work ourselves into a steam with our worry.

One would think that we would have developed a way to shut off all feelings. Goodness knows we have tried. In fact, that's really what addictions do, isn't it? They keep us out of touch with ourselves. And, we can use anything, even worry, to do that. Unfortunately (or fortunately), most of us are like Archie. We get emotionally involved.

Yet, where would we really be without our feelings? Our feelings tell us when there is danger. Our feelings tell us when someone is lying to us. Our feelings tell us when something is wrong. Our feelings tell us that we still have the capacity to love.

We don't really *want* to shut off our feelings. . . . Do we?

Cleaning Our Closets

*When your schedule leaves your brain drained
and stressed to exhaustion, it's time to give up
something. Delegate. Say no. Be brutal. It's like
cleaning out a closet—after a while, it gets easier
to get rid of things. You discover that you really
didn't need them anyway.*

MARILYN RUMAN

When I was a child, I used to listen to Fibber Magee on
the radio. (Strange name, isn't it? As a child I thought
it perfectly normal. I have no idea how to spell it, as I
only *heard* it on the radio.) The most dependable thing
about Fibber Magee was that we knew at some time during every program, he would open this horrendous
closet of his and everything would come tumbling out
on him. He never seemed to remember that his closet
would fall out on him every time but we, the listening
audience, did(!) and we would hold our breath until it
happened.

We are a lot like Fibber Magee. We stuff things in
our minds and in our lives—a huge bunch of festering
feelings, ideas, experiences, and I'll-do-that-tomorrow's.
Those around us are waiting for us to forget and open
the door, knowing it will all come crashing down on us.

**Maybe it's time to sort through the closets of our lives
and have a huge garage sale or giveaway.**

Friendship

*No person is your friend who demands your
silence, or denies your right to grow.*

ALICE WALKER

Being a friend isn't always easy and having friends isn't
easy, especially if we do not do our own work. How often have we abused our friendships by not wanting to
hear the truth about ourselves from those we *say* we
care about? When we demand silence from our friends
and make the friendship conditional upon agreement of
never saying anything we don't want to hear, that isn't
friendship. That is captivity. Our friends, hopefully, are
the people who know us the most. They not only can
see our glaring blind spots, they care enough about us to
tell us—hopefully without judgment.

Also, we cannot be a friend and ask those we love
not to change. How great is our need to get our little
part of the world all fixed up . . . and keep it that way!

*Friends change . . . friendships change. Real friends
move with these changes and talk about them as they
are happening.*

Parenting/Children

Worried parents fail to notice their child's good attitudes.

SUE WHITAKER

Often, when we get obsessed with what is *wrong*, we lose sight of what is *right*. We frequently do this with our children. Sometimes, I think some of us act as if we have children only to provide a focus and an outlet for our anxieties and worrying. What a weight to put on our children!

It's time to shift our perspective. What do we know that is *right* with those persons we have the privilege of rearing? Remember that smile first thing in the morning? Remember the success of those first steps, whether they were the wobbling of a toddler, the dressing up for the first big dance, or the first spark of interest in learning?

Regardless of how many difficulties our children have, real or imagined, they also have many positive accomplishments and *are* many good things. We owe it to ourselves and to them to broaden our focus from time to time. Who knows, this broadening could become a habit.

When I focus only on the negatives with my children, I reduce my world . . . and theirs.

Taking Responsibility

*I enjoy my wrinkles and regard them as badges of
distinction. I've worked hard for them!*

MAGGIE KUHN

Maggie Kuhn was an interesting and challenging
woman. She always was a study in contrasts and surprises. When I knew her, she looked like a petite, delicate cameo, and she was one of the most radical people
I had ever met. The Maggie I knew always took responsibility for her life.

Taking responsibility for our lives is not easy in this
culture. We are trained to be victims. At some very
subtle level, no matter how we have turned out, it is
someone else's fault—parents, of course, are always a
good focus, and teachers, relatives, schools, the church,
and the world in general get their share of blame, too.

It's important to remember that we cannot help
what has happened to us, and many of us have had bad
to horrible experiences. If we want to spend our lives focusing on others and what they have done to us, we can
look forward to a miserable life. Whatever has happened to us is our experience. Our experiences are the
raw materials out of which we can shape a life. What we
build with them is up to us.

**When we recognize that we have worked hard for who
we are—wrinkles and all—we are on the road to being who we can be.**

Open-Mindedness

I worry to save time.

ANONYMOUS

Aren't our minds wonderful! They can turn and twist anything to make it whatever we want it to be. They can get an idea, which may or may not have anything to do with our reality, and they can build on that idea, get ideas from those ideas until pretty soon, we have constructed a virtual reality right in our own heads. Not only that ... we can begin to convince ourselves that the virtual realities that we have constructed are real and we can start living in them, withdrawing and spending little time and energy with those around us.

One challenging and sometimes confusing idea about the human condition is that nothing is ever all good or all bad. Often, what seems like the worst thing that has ever happened to us turns out to be the most important blessing in our lives. For example, I had some friends who lost a child to cancer. I had always thought losing a child to cancer surely was the worst experience a parent could ever have. They did not see it that way—they said her short life and the way she dealt with death were the most profound experiences they had had thus far in life.

Similarly, what looks good at one point may prove to be a disaster later on.

Keeping open minds is a way of staying alive. And staying alive may not be efficient.

Moderation

*I don't know who said it first, but to achieve the
ultimate in happiness one should practice
moderation in all things, including moderation.*
                                    "KUP" KUPCINET

To be moderately moderate in all things can result in
total boredom, especially if our moderation comes out
of our brains and not out of our beings. When we *decide*
to be moderate and leave no room in our lives for
excess, we never leave open the prospect of being ex-
cessively happy.

Certainly as we grow, we learn that many of our
excesses are more trouble than they are worth and we
sigh with relief when the pendulum of our lives settles
from a wildly careening arc to a soft, rhythmic ticking.

The most important thing to notice, however, is
that moderation, like happiness, is not something we
can *control*. Even when we think we are controlling ourselves, it is only a matter of time until that illusion
crumbles. Both moderation and happiness are gifts and
we have only to be ready to be open to receive them.

*When we get to a place where we can practice moder-
ation in all things, especially moderation, we are
probably already happy.*

What's Important

*I confess I am a worrier—and the more
unreasonable the worry, the more likely I am to
lose sleep over it.*

AMY H. BERGER

Who ever said that the things that occupy the greatest
amount of time in our lives are reasonable! Is it reasonable to be hooked by fashion and refuse to wear perfectly good clothes because they are out of fashion? Is it
reasonable to miss the years of our children's growing up
so that we will have a huge estate (or even something!)
to leave them when they are grown?

Is it reasonable that we try to control the lives of
others even after we are dead? Is it reasonable that we
use up more than we produce?

I think not!

Worry is not so different from what we tend to do
with the rest of our lives. When we stop and take stock,
maybe we will see that we are not putting our time and
energy into what really matters for us.

*Perhaps today (April 15—income tax day!) is a good
day to stop and take stock. Are our time and energy
focused upon what is most important to us?*

Goodness

He that has no ill fortune, is troubled with good.

PROVERB

Sometimes things going right almost feels like a burden to us. The pressure almost becomes more than we can tolerate. We are accustomed to the bad things, and we have even developed a certain amount of skill with and acceptance of the ups and downs that we have come to understand as the process of life.

And, when we have a long string of days and weeks when life just purrs along and everything goes fine, we get nervous. The longer it continues the more tense we get. Somewhere, deep inside, we keep waiting for the celestial shoe to fall and are sure that it will. The more nervous we get, the more we begin to pick at little things, pick at our family members, and find fault with those at work. If all this goodness has to come to an end, we feel so much better knowing that we brought the end about ourselves.

Let's face it. We can shore ourselves up. We can stand a lot more good things than we think we can.

When we can "Let Go and Let Life," we can take a lot more goodness than we thought we could.

Frame of Reference

*When I shared with my daughter your idea for a
book on worry, she had no concept how anyone
could not worry. She had no frame of reference
for that at all.*

CHARLEEN

When we consider that at least thirteen million people
in the United States are chronic worriers, it's not surprising that many young people have no frame of reference for non-worry. It's sad to think that we have
created a society where chronic worry is the norm.

What are we teaching our children? Are we teaching them that life is a process and when we live with life
and participate in it, it goes? Are we teaching them that
people should be able to control everything around
them and if they cannot, they are failures? When did
it happen that we began to perceive life as a giant
scientific laboratory in which one should be able to manipulate and control the variables at will?

Have we let our frames of reference become so de-
tached from our experience of life that we are not
teaching our future generations about real life? We are
teaching them about life in a laboratory.

**Luckily for us, nature doesn't know it is supposed to
come under the control of science. We can still learn
about the processes of life there.**

Being Ourselves

I was thought to be "stuck up." I wasn't. I was just sure of myself. This is and always has been an unforgivable quality to the unsure.

BETTE DAVIS

We often experience battering because of our best qualities. I knew a woman once who was very good at loving. She loved easily and well. I'm not talking about a soupy kind of love. I'm not talking about a co-dependent kind of love where she didn't take care of herself and only cared for others. I am not talking about an unclear love where she was being loving only to get something for herself. She just loved in a clean, clear way. This loving was a threat to so many people. Some didn't believe it and wanted to see what the trick was. Some saw it and wanted to turn it into something to make up for all the love they had missed from their parents. Of course, no love can do that. We each have to deal with the experiences we had with our parents. No one can fill us up from outside. When she didn't fix them, they became very angry because they could see the love she had and offered and they still weren't fixed. So . . . they attacked her.

Is it any wonder we sometimes are afraid to admit or show that we are good at something?

Opportunity/Crisis

The Chinese word for crisis is made up of two words—danger and opportunity.

PAGE S. MORAHAN

None of us looks for a crisis in our lives. In fact, we go out of our way to prevent one from happening. In spite of our best efforts, life happens and an occasional crisis happens. Or perhaps it would be better to say, accidents happen, or the unexpected happens. The unexpected, no matter how bad it is, does not necessarily have to be a crisis. It's up to us whether it becomes a crisis or not. We all know people who can make a crisis out of a hangnail or a flat tire.

Some of us have discovered that we feel just as alive without constant crisis in our lives. It is not necessary to give ourselves a rush of adrenaline in order to have the feelings that we interpret as aliveness. In fact, aliveness may have nothing to do with an adrenaline rush.

Whopping up a crisis may, indeed, be dangerous for us and for those around us. We are not present when in a crisis mentality. Yet, if we have learned not to turn the unexpected into a crisis, it is, indeed, filled with opportunity. The real crisis is missing the opportunity . . . for learning.

We don't need a crisis to have an opportunity.

Anticipation

WORRY is often negative anticipation.

BETSY MARTIN

Why are we so drawn to negative anticipation? There are people who believe that if you always expect the worst, then, when something good happens, you are always pleasantly surprised. It's true that very few people worry about something good happening. We worry when we anticipate the worst.

What happens when we anticipate the best? If it doesn't happen, we are disappointed. So? Very few, if any, people have ever died from disappointment. We may not *like* to be disappointed. It's no *fun* to be disappointed. And, it's rarely fatal to be disappointed.

It's hard to believe that we are willing to spend so many hours distorting our lives with negative anticipation rather than take the risk of the luxury of sweet anticipation. Even if whatever we anticipate never happens, we have had the fun of anticipating it and no one can take that away from us . . . no one but we, ourselves, of course.

Negative anticipation robs my present and distorts my future . . . not a good idea.

Self-Reliance

Fear is a sure sign that I am relying upon my own strength.

ANONYMOUS

How unrealistic can you get? I often wonder if we ever fully realize that life is constructed in such a way that it is not possible to live it relying upon our own strength. We simply cannot do it alone. Even if we lived like a hermit in a cave we would have to rely upon the plants and animals for food, and upon air for breathing, and we would have to rely upon the sun and the rain and the earth for growing the things we need. Our own strength is not enough.

City life is even more complex. As we sit down to breakfast, do we let ourselves be aware of the pig who so generously gave his life for our breakfast meat, or the chicken who laid the eggs, or the hands that picked, washed, packed, shipped, roasted, and sold the coffee beans? We are constantly surrounded by reminders that we need much more than ourselves to be where we are.

No wonder we begin to feel afraid when we feel that we are relying only on our own strength. Fear is a realistic emotion in an unrealistic situation.

God

I experience God working in my life. I just wish she/he would show me the business plan.

ANONYMOUS

Dealing with an ever-growing faith is like peeling the layers off a strong onion. We cry a lot, and each new layer is just as strong as the last.

For most of us, faith has not been an easy journey and often it has been complicated by the very institutions that are supposed to know the most about it. Some of us had our Sunday school God. And, often, that God did not wear well over the years. Then, many of us tried to develop an intellectual God or no God at all to fit with our new sophistication. This, too, felt hollow. Some of us pursued the same mental God but sought the other direction and looked for new ideas, new forms of spirituality, and what we call paranormal experiences. Still, often, there was a hollow ring.

Over the years, some of us have come to see and then experience and even admit a power greater than ourselves working in our lives and we respect that power. Still, we would feel better if we just knew where this was going.

Hang on! You ain't seen nothing yet.

Creation

*We are, perhaps, uniquely among the earth's
creatures, the worrying animal. We worry away
our lives, fearing the future, discontent with the
present, unable to take in the idea of dying,
unable to sit still.*

LEWIS THOMAS

What a mess! When we look at what Lewis Thomas has
to say about us, it's difficult to believe that so many of us
suffer under the delusion that we are the end point or at
least the ultimate of evolution. I hope not!

If we let ourselves believe the illusion that we rep-
resent the ultimate of evolution, we put ourselves in the
awkward position of believing that we have nothing
else to learn from the rest of creation, and none of us
really wants to do that now, do we?

After all, there is so much a tree can teach us about
worrying. Or so much a stove can teach us about anxiety. We wouldn't want to miss all these opportunities
for new learnings now, would we?

**When I remember that I am not the creation but only
a part of a much greater whole, I feel a lessening of
pressure.**

Creativity

*Acts of creation are ordinarily reserved for gods
and poets, but humbler paths may circumvent this
restriction if they know how. To plant an oak, for
example, we need be neither god nor poet: one
needs only a shovel.*

ANONYMOUS

We have developed more excuses for avoiding our creativity than for almost anything else in our lives. Most of us have so many fantasies and illusions about creativity and about the products of creativity that we reserve the possibility for people who are definitely not like us.

We imbue our image of creative people with qualities that we could never have, and then require of them that they be eccentric and different from the ordinary if they are truly creative.

The truth is, creativity is everyday. We just don't want to accept that. I knew a man once who was a gifted manager: He was compassionate, efficient, and he gave his employees room to expand and grow while offering them a structure in which to do it. He was good and I loved working for him. But, he did not see good management as creative. He waited to be a conceptual thinker. Sigh!

Creativity is as creativity does.

Energy

*We should look at worry as a manifestation of
nervous intensity, and therefore a potential source
of good. That energy can move us to do the things
that are needed to be done to prepare us for a job
and to do it well.*

REV. LEE TRUMAN

One of my friends used to tell me, "You have a core of
positivism." She always snarled a bit as she said it and I
had some confusion as to whether she saw it as good or
bad. Anyway, I thought it seemed good. However, I
think Rev. Truman has me beat.

Yet, what happens if we think of worry as good?
One possibility might be that thirteen million people
might heave a sigh of relief. (What might that do for
the air quality of the country? We could all benefit!)

If we chose to use the energy created by worry and
change it from potential energy to kinetic energy that
moves us to action, there's no imagining what might be
possible. I remember learning in physics that energy can
neither be created nor destroyed but it can be changed.
Do you suppose that holds in the new scientific paradigm?

**There's nothing good or bad about energy. The key is
in how we use it.**

Isolation

*My mind is a dangerous neighborhood. I should
not wander in there alone.*

ANONYMOUS

Remember Shakespeare's words that "Nothing is either
good or bad but thinking makes it so"? We can think
ourselves into or out of almost anything. Our minds can
be dangerous weapons—especially to ourselves. Most
worriers spend a lot of time in the neighborhood of
their minds *alone*. There is no one in there to help balance our perceptions . . . no one with whom to do a reality check . . . no one to distract us from our galloping
ideas and fears.

Worry is a solitary act. We may share our worries
with those close to us, yet, most of the time we spend with
worry, we spend alone. Worry is like a giant reflective
mirror that bounces back what it receives, with just a few
distortions, GREATLY MAGNIFIED.

*The problem with worrying is, the more we do it, the
more we isolate ourselves. The problem with isolating
ourselves is, the more we do it, the more we do it.*

Remembering

This is the farmer sowing the corn,
That kept the cock that crowed in the morn,
That waked the priest all shaven and shorn,
That married the man all tattered and torn,
That kissed the maiden all forlorn,
That milked the cow with the crumpled horn,
That tossed the dog
That worried the cat
That killed the rat
That ate the malt
That lay in the house that Jack built.

NURSERY RHYME

Remember nursery rhymes? When I was looking for ideas about worry, I ran across a reference to this nursery rhyme. Funny, as my eyes started running across the lines, I had a flood of memories: being read to when I was little; the fun in the singsong rhythm of the lines. In this nursery rhyme "worried" means "pestered." I guess our worries do pester us. Then I went on . . . Jack Sprat . . . I've seen a lot of Mr. & Mrs. Jack Sprats in my life . . . Hickory Dickory Dock . . . how I love my big old grandfather clock. The banging every quarter hour measures the day, and I especially love noon as the big bangs careen through the house.

How much gentler my mind is when it is softly moving through old memories than when it is girdled in worry.

Humor

I have never worried because I have three pets at home that answer the same purpose as a husband. I have a dog that growls every morning, a parrot that swears all afternoon, and a cat that comes home late at night.

MARIE CORELLI

There's something about humor that gets inside us, moves around and through our solar plexus, and tickles our funny bone. I thought it was okay to put this quote about men in because it is funny. Since most comedians are men, we hear a lot of similar jokes about wives.

Regardless of what makes us laugh, none of us can dismiss the importance of laughing at ourselves and, hopefully, being able to laugh at our sacred cows. Actually, it may well be that some secret place hidden deep within us quietly assists in the construction of our sacred cows so that we can trot them out when most needed . . . and . . . laugh at ourselves.

Whenever I start taking myself too seriously, I need to trot out my sacred cows, make a list of them, and read that list to someone near to me who knows how funny and how dear I am.

Seeking Agreement

If I don't worry, who will?

ANONYMOUS

Sometimes we think of worrying in terms of the Hundredth Monkey Syndrome. Scientists doing research on a group of monkeys on a small island theorized that monkeys tended to do things just as they had always done them. Then, one monkey started doing something differently and it worked. Slowly, the other monkeys took up the new way of doing things (big surprise!). At some point when the number of monkeys operating in a new way appeared to reach a critical mass, the new way of doing this activity suddenly jumped to another island. We don't know how this happens or at what point a critical mass is reached. If monkeys can do this, surely we can!

We spend much of our lives trying to gather support. We wander around trying to get other people on our side. If we can just get enough people to agree with us, think like we do, and join forces with us, then we'll be safe. We'll be okay. In fact, many of us firmly believe that if we can just get enough people to side with us, it will prove that we are right.

Who knows? If monkeys can change the world by building a critical mass, maybe we can, too.

Owning Our Past

No man is rich enough to buy back his own past.
OSCAR WILDE

Hopefully, when we look back over our pasts there are a lot of things we would have done differently. That's good! That means we have learned something and the mistakes we have made have not been wasted. However, in order to learn from our past, we have to accept it. We need to see it as our past, our playground for learning.

Luckily, we can't really change our past. Even if we did have the money to buy it back, what makes us so arrogant as to think that we would have the infinite wisdom to make it any better?

Good, bad, or indifferent, our past is the clay we have to work with. We can mold a future that is a vessel to hold our dreams or a cracked pot that leaks them out to seep into nothingness.

Buying back our past isn't a good use for our money anyway.

The Gift of Love

When have I not been dreading dangers more grievous than the reality? Love is a thing replete with anxious fears.

PENELOPE

It's sad, isn't it, that one of the greatest gifts we have as human beings (not that this gift is *exclusive* to humans!), the gift of loving and being loved, is so replete with anxieties. It is difficult to remember that love is always a gift. We cannot make anyone love us no matter how we try. We cannot make our children love us. We cannot make our parents love us. We cannot make our friends love us, nor the man or woman we think we want as a spouse.

The loving itself is not "replete with anxious fears." It is the belief that we can control love that results in anxiety. When we believe that we can control love, we always have to be on red alert, lest in a moment of inattention someone snatches it or it goes away. When it is our responsibility to keep it there, we can never rest.

When I remember that love is a gift, I can relax and enjoy it.

Faith

*Worried that I might never find a rest room, I
wasted much time searching for them while on
vacation.*

AMY H. BERGER

Now, let's face it. It is embarrassing to wet our pants in
public in a foreign country. It's even embarrassing to do
so in our own country! And, most of us have discovered
that anxiety makes us have to go to the bathroom more
often than otherwise.

I travel a lot and I have discovered that shop own-
ers generally can spot an emergency in anxious eyes in
any language. When I have to *go*, I have always found a
place to go . . . behind a car . . . by the side of the road
. . . in an alley . . . in a non-public bathroom. . . . Things
always came out okay, so to speak.

Maybe faith isn't best learned in the "big" issues like
life and death. Maybe faith is best learned in the everyday, in the mundane, in the little insignificant things
that are important to us. Maybe the reason that so many
of us lack faith is that we have tried to jump right to the
big issues without practicing on the baby steps.

**Having faith that I will find a bathroom when I need it
may be the first step toward understanding the meaning of life.**

A Laughing God

If you want to see God laugh, plan your life!

ANONYMOUS

Did you ever think that God may have created the human being for amusement? Perhaps at some point that great celestial being said, "I'm bored. What would amuse me? I would like to see a bunch of creatures who are intelligent and creative and give them free will and see what they do with that." Then God leaned back and took a rest. When God had the time to look in again and see what we were up to, out roared a heavenly belly laugh.

"Why, can you believe that?" God said. "You give them a good mind, creativity, and free will and they think they are in *control*. How do you suppose they got from point A to point B, anyway? I'll just have to watch them awhile and see what they come up with ... Astounding, many of them really believe they are ME. I don't remember throwing that in the bargain." Then God settled back again and decided to watch for a while just to see what we humans were up to.

A giggle here, a snicker there, then a guffaw, there a hoot, or hysterical laughter. Have you heard them?

Respect/Honesty

When my mother worries about me I feel disrespected, like I can't really handle things myself.

KAREN

One of the most important gifts we can give another human being is the gift of respect. Respect is not in high demand nor is it in great supply these days.

Respect is honoring another person's being, whether we like it or not, and recognizing his/her right to be that way. Respect is an awareness of differences that welcomes their existence and anticipates being enriched by them. Respect is not about *allowing* other people to be who they are. It is the recognition that one does not have the right to allow or give permission where other people are concerned. Respect is not giving approval, because no one has the right to approve or disapprove of another. We can have our feelings about what others do, and we do not have approval to give.

Respect is the awareness that others have their lives to lead and that each of us has a personal relationship with the Creator that does not need to be mediated.

When others, especially our children, deal with life differently than we would, or have stressful situations to face, we can respect them by assuming they have everything they need to handle that situation.

Maybe

*About trying on clothes: I worry about whether
I've been the first to try them on. I start thinking
about what horrible disease the last person who
tried them on might have. On those rare occasions
when I've taken underwear into a dressing room,
the rest of the day is shot worrying about germs.*

PAM

There are endless possibilities for worry. I had never
thought of this one. Who ever invented the germs theory
anyway? If we didn't know about germs, we probably
wouldn't have to spend our time worrying about them.
That's the trouble with this information age. We are gen-
erating more information than we can possibly understand, process, or worry about. Of course, this gives us the
unlimited possibility of worrying about what we don't
know to worry about. When we think this way, the possibilities are endless.

I wonder about the old adage, "What we don't
know won't hurt us." We don't know how much our
worry changes the pH level of our bodies and alters the
flow of blood, which carries the white cells that can
fight off the germs that we might or might not have. As
I say, there's great potential here.

**Maybe, when I'm trying on clothes, I could concen-
trate on whether I like them and how they feel on me
. . . just a thought.**

Stopping

Life is a very simple thing. We make it more
complex.

ANONYMOUS

When we are making our life more complex, that is precisely the time when we are totally incapable of seeing
what we are doing. The more complex our lives are, the
more we need to be present to them and, surprisingly,
this is exactly the time when we are most distracted.
When we are distracted, we tend to have poor judgment
and make more mistakes . . . usually adding to the confusion . . . and so it goes.

   Whether we realize it or not, we are totally powerless during these times of confusion. We usually respond
by trying to become even more controlling and, eventually (or immediately!), this just makes things worse.

   It's time to stop, take stock, take some deep breaths,
rest, listen to others, and regroup. Remember that old musical *Stop the World—I Want to Get Off*? Sometimes we
need to do just that. We need to stop our whirl-world and
give it the opportunity to buzz on by us for a while. We
may miss something. We may even miss something we
think is important. That's okay. We're more important.

Taking time to stop may be just what I need to move
ahead.

Happiness

"Don't WORRY, Be Happy!" . . . *It seems that
some folks can't survive without WORRYING; it
may be essential to their "happiness."*

BETSY MARTIN

Maybe some people can't survive without worrying. And
what about LIVING? We often become confused about survival and living. In Western culture, we often look upon
Native peoples around the world who live what we call a
"subsistence" lifestyle as merely surviving. We call them
primitive and are sure they need a more sophisticated
lifestyle and certainly more "things" to make that happen.

I knew a woman a few years ago who bought some
property in Fiji. There was a little all-purpose store on
the property. It was the only one on that end of the island and it operated very simply and effectively. She decided to "beef it up." Later I heard her comment, "You
know, these people don't know what they need. They
didn't even know they needed Saran Wrap until I
stocked it." My guess is, knowing the local villagers,
that they still don't need it.

We would be shocked, sometimes, I think, to realize that there are many people in the world who do not
envy our lifestyle. They think happiness is living their
life peacefully among those they love and having time
for life.

**We have much to learn from others. Happiness is
multi-dimensional.**

Intergenerational

You never can tell when there'll be another depression.

VIRGIL

That's true! You can never tell when there will be another depression. Many of us have grown up with specters that were the hauntings of our parents. The Great Depression has affected many generations in America, even those born long after it. The Second World War is a living legacy in Europe, even to today's young people. It is not only our genes that our parents and grandparents pass on to us.

Often, we take a dualistic approach to our parents and their fears. On the one hand we take on their fears, identify with them, and do our part in an intergenerational worry marathon. On the other hand, we pooh-pooh our parents' fears, think they are silly, tell them they are silly, and refuse to listen to anything they have to say.

There is a third option. We can listen to our parents' stories (we can always learn from our Elders!), listen to their fears and concerns, accept their wisdom, *and* see what we need to do for our own lives.

Worry can be intergenerational without being genetic.

Our Thoughts

One thought fills immensity.

WILLIAM BLAKE

Sometimes I like to think of my mind escaping from my head and moving over the mountains and oceans that guard me, into the immensity of space. I can almost *feel* it moving to the stars and then beyond as it explores possibilities yet unknown to me.

I had a friend once who was very creative and brilliant. I loved to dance with his mind. Whereas mine traveled easily among the stars, I fancied that his often zoomed past mine faster than the speed of light and, without hesitation, plunged right into the black holes of the universe, coming out in places beyond my imagination and far out of my reach. Sometimes, together, we let ourselves travel where neither of us had dared to go alone.

Our thoughts have such possibilities. They can build prisons beyond which we can and will never venture and they can be lasers that cut through the limits of our experience to wisdom beyond ourselves.

It's up to us to accept the challenge of the possibility of our thoughts.

Avoidance/Negativity

Much of my life is arranged around the belief that if I do things just right, I won't have to worry. I guess you would call it a life dedicated to the avoidance of worry.

ANONYMOUS

When we set up our lives to avoid worry, we must somehow assume that worry is inevitable. If we really do believe that worry is inevitable, what makes us think we can control it? If we think that we can control worry by setting up our lives so carefully, why don't we just eradicate it in the first place? That's what's so interesting about so many of the things we try to control: The whole process may be quite logical and rational (given that it is based upon a kind of insanity) and it just doesn't make any sense.

For example, does it really make any sense to set up our lives as an avoidance of anything? Whenever we focus upon avoidance, we are focusing on what we can't do. We are focusing on the negative. Rarely do we realize how much negativity we have in our lives. Negativity has a way of draining the good, leaching out life, and leaving us hollow inside. Negativity has become so commonplace that we have gradually become immune to even noticing it.

When I focus on "the absence of," the present slips away.

Altering Our Minds

*Today I will recognize that worries can be potent
and mind-altering.*

THE COURAGE TO CHANGE

Few of us have recognized worry as mind-altering, but it
is. Worry can be a very effective mind-altering drug.
We also tend to dismiss how powerful it is. Worry is
usually a depressant. And, it is a depressant that is self-
activating and, for some people, progressive.

Worry can produce the same side-effects that we
see in addictions. When we worry we tend to withdraw
from interactions with others (or we worry *when* we are
withdrawn from others!) and we isolate ourselves.
When we worry, we can change our moods ... in-
stantly. When we worry, we tend to become more and
more controlling. Control is almost a knee-jerk reaction
to worry. We also become very self-centered. As we
move more and more into our world of worry, our world
gets smaller and smaller and we tend to believe it revolves around us. In short, we begin to develop some of
the same characteristics of the alcoholic.

These developments do not mean that we are bad
people any more than the alcoholic is a bad person. The
progressive development of these characteristics does
mean that we can use some help.

**If we act like addicts, maybe the program that addicts
use to recover could prove helpful.**

Laughing Brains

I think, therefore I get crazy.

ANONYMOUS

We are a funny lot. I have often wondered about the relationship between seriousness and craziness. As a matter of fact, I have often wondered what the relationship between craziness and craziness is. In my life as a psychologist, I worked in several mental hospitals. Craziness, it seemed, was often a matter of who had the keys. (I always made sure I had mine safe in my hand, I can assure you!) When I actually talked to some of the "inmates," they sounded quite sane and had keen observations. On the other hand, I often had questions about some of my professional colleagues. Sanity, it seemed, was often determined by the point of reference one followed.

Whatever! We have been gifted with a brain that has endless possibilities for creativity. These brains, miraculous though they are, always need a certain chemical produced in the body to keep them in balance. It seems that certain chemicals can only be produced through laughter, and laughter at oneself seems to produce the most potent dosage.

A happy brain is a balanced brain. And a laughing brain is a creative brain.

Saved by Logic

*If the grass is greener in the other fellow's yard—
let him worry about cutting it.*

FRED ALLEN

Of course, if he worries about cutting his grass, is there
some way I can get him worried about cutting my grass?
I mean, if my grass isn't as green as his, maybe he'll get
concerned about my grass and start to take care of it,
since he can clearly see how poorly it's doing. After all,
if his grass is so terribly green, he must have a great investment not only in his yard, he must have an investment in the entire neighborhood. And, if he has an
investment in the whole neighborhood, he must have a
strong need to keep property values up. Therefore, I can
safely assume that the best action for me would be to do
absolutely no yard work for myself so that I can help
him be properly motivated to take care of my lawn so it
will look as good as his.

*Now, isn't life simple? I'm glad I thought that one
through. His house looks pretty good, too, now that I
think of it!*

For Every Season

Things come suitable to the time. Childbirth. An'
bein' in love. An' death. You can't know 'em till
you come to them. No use guessing an' dreading.
ENID BAGNOLD

"You can't know 'em till you come to them." It's so easy
to forget that the passage of time is our friend. When
did we come to believe that time passing is a personal
attack?

Each new stage, each new age, has its own moments. Would we really like to keep our children from
growing up? If they never changed, where would we be
without those wonderful memories that seem so clear to
us in old age?

Would we really want life to be one endless round
of carpooling and scout meetings? How boring to deal
with the same issues over and over again. Life is so constructed that we move through different phases and
stages, each requiring the skills and wisdom of the previous ones.

When I am present to the present I have a future.

Loving Our Children

*When a teenaged child is out at night with friends
and fails to return until an hour or more after the
agreed-upon curfew, the combination of fear and
aggravation experienced by a parent is simply
defined as WORRY.*

BETSY MARTIN

Does parenting ever stop? I doubt it. Perhaps the skills
we learn in dealing with our teenagers are just those we
need to cope with young adults. One of the things we
learn to experience during our children's adolescence is
how important they are to us and how much we love
them. If we didn't care about our children, we wouldn't
experience the fear and aggravation that we feel when
they are late getting in.

Sometimes our primary form of sharing our love for
our children is worrying about them and being aggra-
vated with them when they give us an opportunity to
worry. It helps to remember that when we experience
fear and aggravation, this is an opportunity to show our
love and our caring.

*Love comes in many forms. One of them may be deal-
ing with our own feelings so we can show what's under them to those we love the most.*

Bodies

I have everything I had twenty years ago, only it's all a little bit lower.

GYPSY ROSE LEE

My father used to tell me that I had an hourglass figure but all the sand had sunk to the bottom. He also said that the reason his shirt didn't always quite come together over his paunch was that the doctor had told him to watch his belly.

Many of us have a lot of energy floating around about our bodies. They are either too fat, too skinny, too flat-chested, or too old. There's always something we can focus on . . and focus so easily slips into worry, doesn't it?

What can we do with our bodies, anyway? We can laugh about them like Gypsy Rose Lee. We can recognize that we are responsible for them and they become what we put in them and what we do with them. We can be grateful for their hanging in with us, even if we have made some foolish choices. We can marvel at their ability to heal and rebuild themselves. We can accept them. We can love them.

There is a lifetime of wonders in my body.

Intimacy

*I worry most when I allow myself to love a
person. Sometimes I prefer not to feel love because
then I worry less. I switch between feelings of
distance and feelings of love. Of course I liked the
Janis Joplin song: "Freedom is just another word
for nothing left to lose."*

URSULA

Love has become so difficult and so complex for us humans that we sometimes have come to believe that the only solution is not taking the risk. How sad it is that loving seems like a risk!

We are all so afraid of intimacy that we have, indeed, become a people who actively escape from intimacy. Ironically, it is often those of us who profess the most about wanting to be intimate who are most afraid of it.

Some of us have bought the advertising that sex is the avenue to intimacy, and it just doesn't work. Or we believe that we can become intimate by getting the relationship clearly nailed down. Often this just results in being nailed down. Or we believe that the way to become intimate is to analyze each other so we know "the truth." Often this only results in judgment and frustration.

We forget that intimacy grows and requires time and participation.

Trust

Consider it not so deeply.
WILLIAM SHAKESPEARE

"Consider it not so deeply"
he said
Then turning on his heel
he fled
I'll never know which way
he went
Yet, through the years I
have spent
Much time wondering what
he meant

Perhaps I need to let
things go
A trust in reaping what
I sow
And then at each step I
will know
Assured which way I need
to go.
ANNE WILSON SCHAEF, 1995

Easy, isn't it? Simple, too.

Negativism

When you're an orthodox worrier, some days are worse than others.

ERMA BOMBECK

I guess there's some relief in knowing that no matter how bad things are, they could always be worse. We need to stop and take a look at the way we have let negativism creep into our lives. Negativism is subtle. It's very much like the fog that begins to gather under the cover of night in the low meadows and river valleys as we sleep fitfully in our beds. Unnoticeable at first, it moves along close to the ground in thin wisps barely perceptible to the eye. It moves slowly, rising from the fertile earth and water, changing into a form of its own that we can neither catch nor hold. Slowly, it begins to condense and thicken until we have lost our way in it.

Negativism gathers like fog in our lives and begins to distort our perceptions. We begin to see ghosts and dragons when none are there, and the thicker the negativism, the more we have to rely upon our fertile imaginations to make sense of it.

When we become enmeshed in the fog of our negativism, we have lost our way.

Wisdom

*When our knowledge coalesces with our humanity
and our humor, it can add up to wisdom.*

CAROL ORLOCK

It takes time to develop wisdom. Wisdom requires a
knowledge that is different from information. Information can easily pass through us without ever becoming
knowledge. We can memorize and learn facts without
ever gaining knowledge. Knowledge requires of us an
ability to put the information and facts that we have
gathered together and begin to see the wholes. It is not
possible to have knowledge if we cannot see the wholes.

Then, when we have achieved knowledge, we have
the possibility of nurturing that knowledge with our humanity and our humor. To be human is not such an easy
thing these days. People either are content with being
subhuman and doing and saying things that they know
come from our lower selves or they are busy trying to
be supra-human. To be human means that we fail—
often—and we learn from our failures. To be human
means that we take our place in the whole, and—we do
it laughing.

Wisdom is knowledge that has grown up.

Busyness

Don't hurry, don't worry. You're only here for a short visit. So be sure to stop and smell the flowers.

WALTER C. HOGAN

So many of us spend so much time rushing around that we never even have time to realize we are rushing. Rushing has become a way of life and we become terrorized by the possibility of stopping, having alone time, or just resting. Our busyness has become aligned with our self-esteem and we have come to believe that if we are not busy, we are worthless. Sometimes we even create things to do so we can keep busy.

I wonder if worry is on the mental level what busyness is on the physical level. Could it be that we are afraid of what our minds might do or come up with if we let them be idle and out of our control for a while? Are we afraid of our minds? Are we afraid of mindfulness? Are we afraid of letting our minds go where they will with no guidance from us?

Mental busyness will exhaust us as fast as physical busyness.

Relationships

Whenever I get afraid in relationships I am either
into dishonesty or control.

ANONYMOUS

We have learned that the way to "do" relationships is to focus upon the other person. Most of our "how to's" that we hear as teenagers admonish us to anticipate what the other person wants and needs, get to know what they like and don't like, and try to please them. None of these ideas are bad in and of themselves. It's when we try to use them to manipulate those we love and to control the relationship that we get in trouble.

We also get in trouble when we believe that relationships are built upon focusing on the other person. Because when we focus upon the other person we also tend to focus upon what is wrong with them and what we need to do to fix them or to get them to fix themselves.

Relationships change when we begin to focus upon ourselves and realize that we are the only persons we can change. Do we get afraid? Then let's look at ourselves, see what is going on with ourselves and, when we are clear, share it with the people we love.

When I get clear with myself, I have the possibility of relating to you.

Drugging Ourselves

There are no wonder-drugs for worry, nor will there ever be, short of an anesthetic.

REV. LEE TRUMAN

Ah, an anesthetic. If we could only have an anesthetic to go through life! How lucky we would be never to feel anything, never to know anything, never to be aware of anything, never to worry about anything. Just knock us out and let us get on with life.

How many young women have said, "Just knock me out and let me have a baby when I wake up. I don't want to feel anything."

Medical science has done its best to grant us our fondest wishes. When we have surgery, they offer us a complex set of drugs so that we won't even remember being wheeled into the operating room. Of course, we are never told that this wonderful drug combination may affect the way we function for months to come.

Do we really want to be anesthetized? I doubt it. Do we use worry as an anesthetic? Maybe . . . but it doesn't work, does it?

I'm sure we can find someone who is willing to try to knock out our worry with drugs, and maybe we need to ask ourselves, "Is this what I really want?"

Remember—life is in the living.

Holding On to Hurts

*Don't get your knickers in a knot. Nothing is
solved and it just makes you walk funny.*

KATHRYN CARPENTER

Right! Who wants to get their knickers (underpants,
that is!) in a knot?

Sometimes it's important to get right down to the
basics. Forget about *why* we do what we do. None of this
psychology about "Mother did this"—"Daddy didn't do
that." Just the basics.

Here we are. We are grown people. All kinds of
things may have happened to us as we were growing up.
Sometimes even horrible things. We need to let ourselves know that. We need to work through the feelings
we have from those experiences and learn from them.
And, we need to move on. I have often said, "Victims
never get better. They just get bitter." We may have
been victimized, and when we choose to be victims we
put a halt on our lives.

Each of us has the life we have. It is the clay we
have to work with.

**Holding on to our old wounds is like having a knot in
our knickers. It makes us walk through life funny.**

Facing the Unknown

*I worry about the freeways. If I should go. When
I should go. I tune in several traffic-watch
broadcasts. Then I try to figure out which are the
safest and fastest routes.*

AMY

The choices for worry are endless. Modern life has multiplied the possibilities a millionfold. Freeways offer multiple possibilities and they seem to be getting better and better in that respect.

What person would aimlessly wander out on a California freeway—or any freeway for that matter—without having carefully prepared through pre-worry? After all, we have all been taught that if we are properly and totally prepared, bad things won't happen.

Unfortunately, this approach to life has left us rather weak in the spontaneity department. If something does happen that is not on our list of preparations, we are lost.

We have other options, however.

We can recognize that life is a process and because it is constantly unfolding, we have the opportunity to face the unknown on a daily basis and . . . deal with it.

Now, isn't that a choice thought . . . facing the unknown on a daily basis and dealing with it.

Noticing

*Set up road signs; put up guideposts. Take note of
the highway, the road that you take.*
JEREMIAH 31:21, THE BIBLE

Noticing is one of the most important skills for living.
We can practice on ourselves. We need to learn to notice when we are tired and when we need alone time.
We need to notice what we are feeling and what we
want to do about it.

As we go through life, our noticings can become
our guideposts to come back to so that we can remember what we have learned. Sometimes even we do not
realize at the time that a certain experience may be one
of the most important in our lives. If we notice, if we
put up a guidepost, we can come back to it at a later
time when we have no time to think and can only act.

What is knowledge, after all, but stringing together
the things we have noticed in life? No one else has
taken our particular road and there may be similarities.
If each of us is aware enough to notice the path we take
as we take it, we can share our noticings.

**Some of us need noticing training. Not "figuring out"
training . . . noticing training.**

Habits

*I wouldn't say that I enjoy worrying but I sure
would be lost without it.*

ANONYMOUS

I suppose habits have a place in our lives. I have heard a
lot of people say that they are "creatures of habit" and
that they love ruts. In fact, I have heard several say that
when they fall in a rut they are so comfortable there
that they begin to hang up pictures on the walls!

Habits can be shortcuts that save us time in our
daily living. They can be like old friends who lubricate
our lives. Habits help us become efficient and when we
become efficient, we can have more time to try out new
things.

Unfortunately, habits can become tyrants, too.
They can take on a life of their own and forget that they
are tools that we have invented to smooth our lives.

When our habits take over we need to look at them
closely. If we have come to a point where we would be
lost without them, are we lost with them?

*Maybe today would be a good day to take a "habit" in-
ventory and go over it with someone we trust (someone other than ourselves, that is).*

Spending Our Gifts

*God never built a Christian strong enough to
carry today's duties and tomorrow's anxieties piled
on the top of them.*

THEODORE LEDYARD CUYLAR

God probably never built anyone that strong, Christian
or not.

Why is it that we always seem to be pushing ourselves? Instead of spending our time trying to let ourselves know what we were created to be and what we
are created to handle, we spend our time trying to push
ourselves beyond our limits.

What would our lives be like if we only took on
what we could comfortably do? What if we stopped before every new opportunity and gave ourselves time to
sit with the option and see if it is right for us at that
time and in that place? What if we approached life as a
great gift that we do not want to spend foolishly on
tempting trinkets and baubles? What if we saw life as
ours to spend in the way that would be most beneficial
to our spiritual growth? Would we be piling anxieties on
today's duties?

*If I take true responsibility for my life, would I be do-
ing what I am doing now? If not, I'd better reconsider.*

Imagination

Worry is nothing less than the misuse of your imagination.

ED FOREMAN

Our imaginations . . . what wondrous gifts they are! Did you ever just sit down and imagine all the colors you could? Not just those you have seen . . . Can you imagine those you haven't seen? Difficult, isn't it?

Or, have you ever imagined a new species of animal? What would you make?

Every day I use my imagination in much more mundane ways and even though they are simple, I enjoy them.

For example, one of my favorite "creativity's" is to walk into a kitchen where the refrigerator and the pantry seem empty and create a gourmet meal. Or, I especially like taking some leftovers and combining foods that are not usually combined to make a memorable dish.

Also, I have lots of clothes and I always get a thrill when I put together a costume I had never even considered and it looks great! (Sometimes outlandish and *great*!)

Creating with the ordinary is sometimes the most creative act of all.

Memories

Happiness is good health and a bad memory.
INGRID BERGMAN

Memory can be a conundrum. We really know very little about it when you get right down to it. We can distort memories to fit our purposes. Sometimes we even get away with it because we are the only ones who know. Psychologists believe we can have false memories even when we have body memories to go with them.

We can have sense memories, too. Even when we don't have words, we can remember a taste of chicken and noodles our friend's mother made when we were a child, the feel of plunging into a cold swimming pool on a hot summer day, the touch of a hand on our hair, or the smell of a deep woods after a rain. These memories enrich our lives.

Memories are part of us and the life we have lived. Maybe it is not necessary to have a bad memory to be happy if we trust that our inner being will present us with the memories we need when we are ready for them. If we can trust our inner being we can relax anyway.

Maybe happiness is good health and *a selective memory.*

Knowing Another

Sometimes you have to get to know someone really well to realize you're really strangers.
MARY TYLER MOORE

Do we ever really know another person? And what is another person? We have come to believe that a person is a person and that person is static. Since we do not expect her or him to change, we believe that once we get to know them, that's it. We can relax and move on to other things.

But, what is a person? If we think of a person as a series of changing processes which overlap, interact, intertwine, and intersect, we have a much different concept of getting to know someone.

From the above perspective, a person becomes a combination of never-ending, ever-changing processes in which we can participate. And, of course, our participation changes the processes of the other and their processes change ours. Imagine, if you will, two flowing, constantly changing kaleidoscopes merging with and separating from one another and then you have a sense of what relationships could be like if we trusted them.

Maybe knowing another person is a lifelong process and not a task to be accomplished.

People Who Don't Worry

I can't remember the last time I worried.

RODDY

Sounds great! Either he has a bad memory or he doesn't worry much, or both.

Are there really people in this world who don't worry? What do people do who don't worry? Surely, responsible people worry. How can they be responsible if they don't worry?

What are people like who don't worry? Do you suppose they live down the block or up the street? Surely, they cannot be anyone we know very well.

When we think about it, don't we sort of resent people who don't worry? It's like they aren't carrying their share of the load, isn't it? It's like they are leaving all the responsibility to us and are getting off scot-free doing just what they please. Why, they might even be taking advantage of our worrying. It's not fair. How can they do that? There ought to be a law. People like that should be locked up somewhere so that good responsible people like us wouldn't have to take care of them.

When you get right down to it, I think not worrying should be a crime. Don't you?

Attention

Energy goes where attention flows.

PROVERB

We tend to send our energy where our attention is. Unfortunately, not all energy is positive. And when we send our energy in a negative way, we may well send those we love negative energy without even realizing it.

We may call it concern, worry, or care and when it is negative, the attention may not accomplish what we want. For example, children whose parents worry about them a lot often feel untrusted and act accordingly. Employees whose bosses worry about what they are doing may feel watched and progressively lose interest in their job. The attention we are giving may not bring about the desired effect.

It doesn't really do much good to try to change the energy we are sending others through our will. We may, however, let our attention wander to the good things they are doing. When we start looking for things we can applaud, we may begin to see them.

Remember, our attention affects those we attend to.

Participation

*I feel sorry for people who don't worry. How do
they get prepared?*

ANONYMOUS

Just what are we preparing for anyway? When we see
worry as preparation, we may be preparing for the
worst. We may even believe that if our worry is good
enough, we can keep bad things from happening. And,
even if we can't keep them from happening, we will be
prepared.

There is, however, a different way to look at preparedness. What if we were prepared for good things to
happen? We can anticipate meeting someone we like
whom we haven't seen for a long time. We might even
see that it happens. We might prepare for life to unfold
in new directions which are, as yet, unimagined by us.
We might trust it will be the right solution.

*We can choose to have faith and when we have faith,
we are prepared for anything.*

Sharing Foibles

I'm completely exhausted from all the problems I have at my job, which doesn't start until next Monday.

PETE

Aren't we funny? Nobody will ever know how really funny we are if we don't tell jokes on ourselves. Only we have the information to give detailed reports of the crazy ways our minds work and the latest grand scheme we have concocted. How wonderful it is to share these little secrets about ourselves with those close to us and have a good laugh together.

Sharing our little daily insanities is a great way to develop intimacy. Nothing is more endearing than a sentence that begins with, "Well, guess what I did to-day—You'll never believe it—I couldn't," and goes on from there.

So often we have hesitated to share these "secrets" because we wanted to maintain some image that we *thought* we had, not realizing that supporting the image was an escape from intimacy itself.

Those who care about us love to hear the truth about us . . . especially when it's funny.

Sharing myself is easier than I thought and it helps a lot if I am the first one to laugh.

Feeling Feelings

Worry is the thinking part of anxiety.
                    AMY H. BERGER

I wonder what would happen if we just stuck with the anxiety? Anxiety is a feeling and, in general, I have come to believe that feelings are our friends. Feelings let us know where we are in time and space and often are the only clues we really have about who and where we are.

There are no such things as "negative feelings." It is what we do with feelings that makes them negative.

For example, we often feel anxiety in relation to our children. If we did not care, we would not feel anxiety. The problem comes when we move from our guts and our hearts to our brains. If we just sit with the feelings we are having in our hearts and our guts, we usually discover that while the anxiety we are feeling may be triggered by our children, it often has something to do with issues that have been unresolved in us. Our children and their issues only provide us with the door to walk through to our own healing.

When I focus on others, I may be trying to avoid what's going on with me.

Keep Moving

*I find the great thing in this world is not so much
where we stand as in what direction we are
moving.*

OLIVER WENDELL HOLMES

When we become obsessed with where we stand, we
may be incapable of moving. So much of the current
self-help literature encourages us to know ourselves and
to know what we believe and why. Since so many of
us in this culture have defined ourselves from outside
and know little of who we are and what we like, this
self-definition is an important process. We learn to set
boundaries and limits. We have definition.

Yet, what's going on here? Those very same characteristics that resulted in our being boundaryless now exercise their muscles in setting boundaries that *are* not
only boundaries . . . they are steel-reinforced concrete
walls that are four feet thick and are taking on the image of a prison. We are not only taking a stand as to
who we are, we are setting boundaries that even we cannot penetrate. We cannot move because we have constructed a rigidity that is truly as isolating and static as
our lack of boundaries.

When only the surface changes, nothing changes.

Problem-Solving

*Worried parents don't know how to teach their
children to solve problems.*

SUE WHITAKER

Life is a risk. That's the truth of it. If the purpose of living
is to do it (life, that is), anything we do that keeps us from
"doing it" is actively working against the purpose of life.

Most of us get the big lessons from doing. We can
try to think something out ahead of time (of course, trying to imagine all the exigencies!). And, we can try to
anticipate everything our children need to know so that
they can live the perfect life (generally one that does
not look like ours!). Yet, when we get right down to it,
most of what we really need to learn, we learn through
experience.

Often, when we are worried about someone else,
we start behaving in such a way as to decrease our own
anxiety and worry. Frequently this worried behavior
translates into trying to prevent anything from happening to those we love, and eventually results in a lack of
life-skill training and an inability to solve one's own
problems.

*The great thing about being a parent is, you're
damned if you do and you're damned if you don't. Better just let go and live with our kids, I guess.*

Surprises

When I was six I made my mother a little hat—
out of her new blouse.

LILLY DACHÉ

One of the characteristics of this life is that we rarely know the meaning of events as they happen. In fact, events may find their meaning in the attitude we bring to them.

We often lose the possibility of experiencing our lives when we do not have the patience to wait with an event and learn its meaning for us over time. It is surprising how much power we have to determine the ultimate meaning of past events. One thing is certain. We cannot determine this evolving meaning with our thinking.

Ultimately, it is our openness to the serendipities of life's lessons that will make the difference.

After all, only time will tell us what a hat made out of a new blouse can evolve into!

The disasters of the past may be the successes of the future.

Definitions

While taking Dolly to the airport we stopped at a store to buy her water for the plane trip. The store was closed. I felt scared because I didn't know any other stores on the way to the airport, and we had no extra time to look off of our airport route. I prayed: "God help us find water for Dolly." Just then Dolly looked at me and asked if she could have some of my water. I said yes—but I've drunk out of the bottle a lot, refilling it each time.

She then reached down on the car floor and brought up a large unopened bottle of water which I'd forgotten was there! Immediate answer to prayer—which I said—followed by, "We didn't have to worry. . . ."

CONNIE

There are times when we begin to become aware of the funny little ways in which we have learned to define our lives: "I need to worry about that one." . . . "That's not worth worrying about." . . . "I didn't have to worry about that." . . . "If I don't worry, it won't happen." . . . "Worrying shows that I care." . . . "I don't have time to worry about that."

Or, our lives become defined in terms of stress. Or, our lives become defined in terms of "I can't." Our lives become defined in terms of worry.

We'd better watch the definitions of life that have *us*.

Strength

*We deceive ourselves when we fancy that only
weakness needs support. Strength needs it more.
A straw or a feather sustains itself long in the air.*
ANNE SOPHIE SWETCHINE

We often deprive those we know and care about of support because we see them as strong and able to take care of themselves. Frequently it is the strong and the capable who get the most battering. People take one look at a strong person and assume that "they can take it."

We often think that those whom we admire and who are out there paving the way for us could not possibly need the support of "someone like us."

How wrong we are!

The people we lean on would be so grateful for a little support from us. We can spare it.

Skills

Worry never robs tomorrow of its sorrow; it only saps today of its strength.

A. J. CRONIN

We cannot worry tomorrow into being. It will come on its own, often bringing surprises that are beyond imagination. If there is sorrow tomorrow, we will have to deal with it then. However, when we use today to practice dealing with the sorrows that may erupt tomorrow, we not only do not develop any usable skills; we may miss today in the process.

How often do we rob ourselves of the daily activities that could build our strength because we are holding our breath about tomorrow. If sorrow comes tomorrow, we may well need the strength of today to cope with it.

Strengths are transferable. Todays are not. I may be so focused upon tomorrow that I miss the training in the exact skill I will need tomorrow. Life is like that.

Sorrow practice has never proved to be effective.

Quarrels

It takes two to make a quarrel, but only one to end it.

PROVERB

Years ago, when I was a psychotherapist, I used to listen to couples trying to sort out their quarrels. There was often the "You said . . . I said" phase, followed by the favorite forms of unseemly accusations, which I would monitor as I attempted to support the couple in their sorting out.

Yet, over time, I saw how fruitless all this activity was. I began to see that most quarrels happen because something the other person says or does triggers us and we actively, and with the righteousness of surety, focus on what they have done. We have learned not to take responsibility for our *reactions*.

The other person may be a complete schmuck in this instance. That's none of our business. They have to live with that!

Our reaction is our business. AND, it is the only part of this scenario we can do something about.

Evaporation does not happen just to water: It's surprising what happens to quarrels when both people deal with themselves.

Designated Worriers

*My Aunt Rea worries for the whole family so I
don't have to worry about worrying.*

BARB

The problem with this world is that we just do not have
enough Aunt Reas for every family!

Imagine the world of the future where one person is
selected from each family and is especially raised and
trained to be the expert worrier. These worry skills would
be very valued by the society and the selected worriers
would be freed of the actual tasks of living because they
were deemed to be necessary for the functioning of the
society.

Actually, the designated worrier would take on the
worries for a specific number of persons. If the families
were too big, which, of course, they rarely would be because the size of families would be limited, they would
have to have more than one trained worrier.

Once the worrying function had been cornered, it
would be illegal for others to worry because it would dras-
tically interfere with their productivity. Non-worriers
caught worrying would be arrested and heavily fined. The
third offense could result in death.

Don't worry! (Unless you're supposed to!)

Who's in Charge Here?

*We come and go but the land is always here. The
people who love it understand this.*

MAORI ELDER

Native peoples are always tied to the land. Their identity, their meaning, their spirituality, and their security
are tied to the land.

After spending so much time with Native people, I
have noticed that those who live closer to the land and
accept that they have no control over the processes of
nature live serenely.

I often wonder if so much of our modern anxiety
stems from our disconnectedness from the processes of
the universe. Perhaps, if we stop and really let ourselves
know that we are part of a larger picture over which we
have no control and in which we can participate, we
will relax.

**When I know I'm not in charge, I can let one who is
more qualified take over.**

Doing What We Do Well

Worrying is serious business. It shouldn't be left to amateurs.

ANONYMOUS

In this life, one of the most important discoveries we can make about ourselves is learning what we are good at doing.

Mediocrity for most of us is not a challenge; it is a settling. And even if we settle for the daily tasks we have to do, it is also important to know what we do well.

All of us have skills. To some, they may not seem like skills at all . . . but they are. Even if we cannot support ourselves financially with our best skills, we need to notice them, appreciate them for what they are, and practice them when we can. Indeed, if we are really good at them, they will contribute something to ourselves and our community.

I, myself, am an amateur worrier—I'd best leave it to the experts.

Letting Go

Take things as they come.

PROVERB

Now really! Isn't this silly? Proverbs are supposed to be the wisdom of the culture condensed in a few words. This is like "One Step at a Time." Did you ever try to take two steps at a time? . . . or three? . . . or four? Well, we can see how silly that is, can't we?

Now, how can we possibly not take things as they come? Can we take them *before* they come? I doubt it. Can we *not* take them when they come? Some try, and usually set themselves up for failure, which is great for the self-esteem. Can we try to make things happen on our time schedule? This usually requires much more power and control than mere mortals can muster.

I mean, really. What's a person to do?

Could it possibly be that participating in the unfolding of our lives is really all we have to do?

Fooling Ourselves

*A person must try to worry about things that
aren't important so he won't worry too much
about things that are.*

JACK SMITH

Fooling ourselves seems to be a national pastime. How
dumb do we think we are anyway?

We spend so much time trying to create subterfuges
for ourselves that we think nothing of it when others do
the same thing . . . and say they are telling the truth.
We have trained ourselves not to recognize illusions in
ourselves or others. We must remember that no one can
fool us unless we are willing to be fooled. However, our
penchant to fool ourselves has set us up for easy fooling
by others. We have become sitting ducks.

We are the only ones who can keep ourselves from being fooled.

Interpretation

The reason some men fear older women is they
fear their own mortality.

FRANCES LEAR

Instead of dealing with our own feelings with regard to another person, we often use interpretation as an escape from intimacy. What happens to us inside as older women when we experience some men fearing us? When I let myself be aware of what I am feeling when I read these words, I feel sadness—sadness that I may not be seen as an individual and only as an "older woman." I feel frustration—frustration that there is probably nothing I can do to break through that other person's wall of perception to be just the two of us, facing each other as people. I feel anger that I am being put in a box not of my own making and over which I have little influence. Honoring myself as I do, I can easily move behind the anger to my feeling of helplessness in not being able to control or change others. Ah, there's the red flag!!

When I feel helpless or powerless, my backup style is a knee-jerk response to try to regain "control" and spew a little of my anger out in the process. Interpretation is the perfect tool for this process. Unfortunately, interpretation destroys the possibility for intimacy.

When I stop and ask myself if I really want to escape from intimacy, the answer is almost always no.

"Worrying" Our Lives

*I immediately remembered your response in your
last letter—"Don't get addicted to the struggle"—
I've wondered how I can worry so much and have
a marvelous life!*

CHARLEEN

Like almost anything else, worrying can become a habit
that slips into an obsession.

Why can't human beings "leave well enough alone"?
Even if our lives and the lives of those around us are
pretty good, we seem to need to "worry" them. We treat
our lives like the little holes we had in our clothes as children. Remember when we would find a loose thread in
our favorite pair of pants? It wasn't a hole yet . . . just a
thread loose. And we couldn't leave it alone. We picked
at it. We pulled at it. Our attention kept drifting back to
it and we tugged and pulled until it became a full-blown
hole. Then we went running to our mommies, crying
that our favorite pants were on the brink of destruction.

*The skill of making a hole out of a loose thread is not
necessarily a good skill for living.*

Mistakes

A mistake is an event, the full benefit of which has not yet been turned to your advantage.

ED LAND

Mistakes don't just happen. We make them. Often, the real challenge of the mistake comes long after the actual mess-up. It's up to us to glean the learning from the mistake.

Quite often, in fact, mistakes may have many learnings and the pursuit of those learnings may be an unfolding process that takes place over many years. During the process of gleaning the learnings, we may go down many false alleys and draw several wrong conclusions. That's okay. Also, friends may be more than eager to tell us what we should think and feel about the mistake, and may chide us for some learnings that they think are wrong. In the end, however, it is up to us to do the work that turns the full benefit of the learning to our advantage.

Important learnings take time.

Decisions

Once a decision was made, I did not worry about it afterward.

HARRY S. TRUMAN

Good ol' Harry! . . . and he made some whoppers!

Perhaps, ultimately, the decisions that we make are not what's most important. *Living the consequences of those decisions* is the true challenge. The decisions, once made, cannot be undone. The process of worrying about the decisions after they are made is one of the ways we try to hedge on the decision.

Unfortunately, when we put ourselves in the position of hedging upon a decision, we rob ourselves of dealing with the consequences of the decision and of owning our lives. When we second-guess ourselves, we place ourselves in a kind of limbo where continuing with our lives is impossible and maintaining a static existence consumes all our time and energy.

Living with our decisions is the grist for life's learning mill.

Fringes

The hardest years in life are those between ten and seventy.

HELEN HAYES

Sometimes it's the fringes that really count. It is so easy to forget about the fringes of our lives because we tend to focus our attention on the "hard" or the "important." Maybe something only becomes important because we give it our attention. The more we focus our attention on what is hard, the less time and energy we have to appreciate the herbs and spices of living.

Take the years between one and ten, for example. We probably gain more knowledge during that period than any other time in our lives . . . perhaps because we have not learned to focus and have been able to let the fringes into our imaginations and our curiosity. And, maybe it gets easier after seventy because we know better.

What I make into fringes in my life may actually be the spices I need for living.

Living in Our Own Minds

Worrying supports the addictive system. When I worry what someone else is thinking of what I am doing, my disease is sending out an engraved invitation to their disease. What a surprise to find out that they are minding their own business!

DOLLY

How often do I send out engraved invitations for people to beat me up? Am I actively eliciting that which I fear the most? It's not that I can control what others think or don't think of me *and* I can take responsibility for inviting them into my mind and soul.

Maybe it's time to give some thought to what it means to invite others into our minds and souls . . . for once they get in there, we have little or no control over what they do there. They can build mansions, set up housekeeping, and bring their relatives in, all at our invitation.

When it gets right down to it, it is really none of our business what others think about us or what they say about us. We have no control over either.

It is, however, up to us whether we send out engraved invitations to move into our minds.

When I worry about what others say about me or think about me, I am printing up invitations for taking up residency in my mind.

Blessings and Curses

Every blessing ignored becomes a curse.
PAULO COELHO

Life is a series of blessings. They are bestowed upon us daily in profusion and in such a variety of ways that it boggles the mind. In fact, it may be because of this boggling of the mind that we fail to see them.

Can it be that we, ourselves, have the power to turn the blessings of the universe into a curse? Is it possible that we are so busy living day to day that we ignore blessing after blessing?

Today may be a dark, cloudy, rainy day. We had hoped for sunshine. Is this a way of turning a blessing into a curse? Cloudy, rainy days give us a chance to slow down ever so slightly. Do we need that today?

A proposal we have worked on long and hard was just rejected. Perhaps we cannot see the blessing yet ... *and* it is important to be open to the blessing hidden inside.

Perhaps I don't always have the wisdom and the support of the passage of time to see the current blessing and it is best not to ignore the possibility.

Preparation

*If you worry enough about all the terrible things
that can happen, at least you're prepared.*

ANONYMOUS

So much of our lives is spent in preparation. We have
come to believe that if we can just prepare for every
possibility, nothing bad can happen *or* we can *keep* anything bad from happening. Preparedness has become a
national buzzword. Yet, at some level we have to recognize that what we are doing is really magical thinking.
We come to believe that it is the *preparedness* that keeps
bad things from happening.

I am reminded of an old African story. One day a
tourist was passing through a village and asked a villager, "Why do all the huts have pieces of red cloth
hanging by their doors?" "That is to keep tigers away,"
answered the villager. "But there are no tigers in this re-
gion," said the tourist. "See!" said the villager.

**Who knows what works? At least one thing is sure. If
we focus our energies on being prepared, we'll be prepared—for something.**

Respectability/Cons

The more things a man is ashamed of, the more respectable he is.

GEORGE BERNARD SHAW

In the future, will today's people be seen as a group who lived their lives so as not to be caught?

At some point in our lives, we have to stop and ask ourselves, "What can we truly trust in ourselves?" Are we really the people we present to ourselves and others? How far do our "cons" go? Are we willing to stop and take a look at our "cons" and try to get honest with ourselves?

Conning is one of the most deadly games we can play with ourselves and others and, even though our conning always results in a destruction of the true possibility of relationships, the person we hurt most is ourselves.

We are always the ones most fooled by our own cons and we rob ourselves of knowing ourselves, which is always an ultimate loss of our lives.

I'm much better off dealing with my shame than trying to bury it in fake respectability.

Spirituality

Worry is a thin stream of fear trickling through the mind. If encouraged, it cuts a channel into which all other thoughts are drained.

ARTHUR SOMERS ROCHE

Like water on sandstone, worry moves through our minds and beings and creates canyons into which we can fall without knowing it.

Perhaps we can start to see ourselves as spiritual civil engineers who can begin the enormous job of filling the grand canyons in our minds.

The lovely thing about spirituality, however, is that it is not confined to the mechanistic material world that we call reality. Spirituality can expand or contract as the occasion demands, move around corners, become any form needed, and fill all the crevices within us.

Our spirituality is not something we have to find or even understand. It is always there, slumbering within us, awaiting our noticing.

Spirituality is like one of those little cups of soup that says "add water" and it expands into a meal. All we need to do is add attention.

Feelings

Feeling my feelings is the most spiritual thing I can do.

KAREN

In this modern world, we have come to think of feelings as unimportant and bothersome. We spend a good deal of time trying to ignore and repress them. And we feel put upon and annoyed when they don't just quietly go away when we want them to.

How differently we might look upon them if we believed that feeling our feelings is the most spiritual thing we can do! Is it part of the Creator's grand design for the human being that we can never quite completely control our feelings? What if our feelings are, indeed, the door into our spirituality and without them we lose our way?

When we feel our feelings, we bypass the illusion of control of our rational mind and move into the unknown, where the usual techniques to keep us out of touch with the process of creation just do not work. Our feelings provide us not only with a door but also with a pathway to return to that which is beyond our thinking.

Feeling my feelings is not the same as acting out my feelings. Feeling feelings is a return to spirituality.

Thinking

*In order to draw a limit to thinking, we should
have to be able to think both sides of this limit.*
LUDWIG WITTGENSTEIN

Right! It is only when we think about thinking that we
can truly have the experience of thinking. Yet, the experience of thinking can't possibly be *real* thinking because true thinking cannot afford to be contaminated
by experience or it loses its purity. (Whew!)

Therefore, when we think about both sides of drawing a limit to thinking, we discover that by setting up
the limit as something with two sides, we have thrown
our thinking into a dualistic model, and our thinking
tells us that there are basically two purposes to setting up
a dualism. Those purposes are: 1) to maintain the illusion of control by setting up an oversimplified dualistic
system which is illusionary and calling it real, and 2) to
stay stuck.

Therefore, when we want to draw a limit to thinking by setting up an illusionary dualistic thinking
process which assumes two sides, we have to indulge in
a great deal of thinking to ascertain which are the *real*
two sides of the limit. . . . So there!

**One thing about thinking . . . there's no room to
limit it!**

Peace

WATER SPIRITUAL

A waterfall's
A lovely place
To sit awhile
And know God's grace

Plunging home
To the sea
Oblivious to you
Unseeing of me

The water knows
Which way to go
Returning to the sea
It must be so

It's not too complex,
This water song
It just keeps moving
Right along

No care for this
For that, no thought
Life is so simple
We'd almost forgot

I sometimes wonder
What point did we
Forget to notice
Life could be free

To move like water
T'ward our home
Is an easy task
Not done alone

The Creator's grace
Accompanies us
We're not forgotten
This, we can trust

To worry is only
As we all know
A lack of faith
In what is so

To move like water
Powerful yet weak
Will bring us to
The peace we seek

ANNE WILSON SCHAEF, 1994

Our teachers are all around us.

Contentment

Take care and go gently and contentedly on with doing good work.

JOHN CASTEEL

"Doing good work" seems so old-fashioned, doesn't it? Well, John Casteel was an old-fashioned man. He was one of the few Renaissance men I ever knew and he died recently in his nineties, having gone "gently and contentedly . . . doing good work" all his life.

What comes to mind when we think about being gentle and contented? Gentleness is something I always see in the Elders. It is as if they have learned that banging and smashing through life isn't what life is really about. Gentleness breeds gentleness and invites a living "with" ourselves, each other, and the planet.

Contentedness—this is a word that has fallen into disuse in contemporary society. To be contented with our lives on a moment-to-moment basis . . . to accept them as they are . . . and to let go of the endless striving even for a moment leads to contentment. Contentment is like the celestial sigh that reorganizes our lives and puts them in perspective.

And, lastly, doing good work—how much better we feel about ourselves when we are doing good work— work that has meaning for us and the planet.

The work that I do gently out of contentment feels different somehow.

Isolation

Worry is love. How will your children know you love them if you don't worry about them?

ANONYMOUS

What we really want to do is love our children and let them know that we love them.

So often we are afraid of loving. We are afraid that we won't do it right or that our love will be rejected. Many of us feel that we have not had good models for loving and we really don't know how to do it. And, who wants to risk doing something when we aren't sure we can do it well?

One option we have is to be honest. We could just tell the truth and tell our kids that we want to love them and we don't quite know how to go about it. This honesty could work.

After all . . . nothing ventured, nothing gained.

Negative Thinking

*Alas! my friend, there appears to be a strange
propensity in human nature to torment itself, and
as if the physical inconveniences with which we
are surrounded in this world of ours were not
enough, we go forth constantly in search of mental
and imaginary evils—This is nowhere so
remarkable as among those who are in what we
call affluence and prosperity. . . .*

CHARLOTTE SMITH

Does leisure bring worry? I don't know. Are we surrounded by physical inconveniences? I don't know. Perhaps having to deal with a physical body and a physical universe is inconvenient. I don't know. Actually, I kinda like it myself. I never cease to be astounded by the ability of the human body to heal and bounce back even after terrible trauma. Or, have we ever stopped and noticed how much physical abuse our bodies take and they still keep going?

Or, did you ever notice that we have birds who still sing and plants that still bloom in spite of our attempts to pollute the planet?

Perhaps the real inconvenience we have to deal with is our negative thinking.

Spiritual Freedom

*The freedom now desired by many is not freedom
to do and dare but freedom from care and worry.*

JAMES TRUSLOW ADAMS

Freedom! The very word makes us want to stand up straight, hold our heads up high, and start marching to some patriotic song. Yet, what kinds of freedom do we most cherish? Political freedom?—Yes, of course. In some ways that is the easy one and usually the one that gets our attention on this day or any day.

Yet, the freedom that undergirds our very being is spiritual freedom—not just religious freedom, which is, indeed, important—but—spiritual freedom.

Spiritual freedom is freedom to live our values and our beliefs. Spiritual freedom is the freedom to nourish our souls, trust that "still small voice" within us, and live out that which feeds our spirit. Spiritual freedom is the peaceful knowing that we are not in charge nor do we need to be. Spiritual freedom is the freedom of living in full participation with the Creator while being present to our lives.

Spiritual freedom is, indeed, freedom from care and worry.

Blame

Blame keeps wounds open. Only forgiveness heals.

WILLA CATHER

Part of our problem with blame is that we often use it as an end point when it should, in fact, exist only at the very beginning of a process, if at all. Our tendency to blame others can be a red flag that there is something going on that we need to look at. For many of us, our knee-jerk reaction is to look for someone to blame. We may even focus upon ourselves as a good "blame object" and in that process, objectify ourselves just as we objectify others.

Hopefully, we can soon see that blame is irrelevant and the issue is not who or what to blame. The issue is to stop and see what we are feeling and see what we need. When we realize that we can focus on ourselves, and see that often we move to blame when we are unsure of the feelings beneath the blame or what to do with them, then we can back off and see what we need.

Only when we honor what we need will forgiveness follow.

Travel

I try to get to the airport very early so I won't
have to worry about being late.

ANONYMOUS

Travel offers endless opportunities for worry! Those of us who tend to worry have somehow developed a belief in the direct relationship between arriving early, safety, and freedom from worry. Therefore, if we get to the airport only an hour early, we are going to have to cope with at least an hour's worth of worry to make up for the fact that we would have had to worry less if we had been able to get there two hours early.

Of course, this particular formula only relates to catching the plane (which *could* leave early, you know, even though this is an unknown event in the life of air travel). When we get there very early, we have time to sit around and think about other things we might worry about: Will our luggage get on the right plane? Will someone steal it between check-in and the plane? Will it be damaged? Will someone else be assigned to our seat? Will we get the seat we want? Will we be seated next to a huge bore? Will—will the plane crash?

There are so many possibilities for mishaps involved in travel, we might as well let it go and turn this complex mess over to our Higher Power.

Choices

I can choose my response—and I can't control what's happening.

MIA

Choosing our response and knowing that we cannot control what is happening is one of those little lesson gems in life that can make the difference between chaotic stress and living serenely.

Often, the little key that opens the big door is nothing more than a slight shift in perception. It is comforting to know that this shift in perception takes place within us and nowhere else.

Other people, ultimately, will do what they want. We can't control that. Events will happen. We can't control that. Institutions will rarely function the way we want them to. We can't control that. Life, thank goodness, never quite follows our master plan. We cannot make it so.

We do, however, have a choice as to how we respond to these "uncontrollable" events. *And*, we even have a choice as to how we respond to our initial response.

When I choose how I respond, I am not controlling. I am just exercising my prerogatives.

Normalcy

Like traffic jams, flat tires, headaches and cramps,
housework, cold sores, messy diapers, and gray
days; the worry habit makes problems worse.

SUE WHITAKER

Part of our difficulty in dealing with traffic jams *et al* is that we have come to view them as unusual. Somewhere along the line we failed to notice that life is.

In our illusionary approach to our lives we have been able to fool ourselves into thinking that things should go *right* and . . . we have a very specific idea of what "right" is. We have come to believe that the easy, the problemless, the fun are "normal" and everything else is abnormal or bad. We have predetermined what life is or should be and we expect it to run smoothly along those lines.

Well, surprise! Life happens. When friends or family die, when we go through a bad period, we just want things to get back to normal. Well, this is "normal." This is what life is and we have the choice of participating in all of it as normal.

Our idea of "normal" and "not-normal" has caused us
a lot of pain.

Meditation

Half an hour's meditation is essential except when
you are very busy. Then a full hour is needed.

FRANCES DE SALES

I suppose when meditation moves from being a luxury to being a necessity we have truly begun to start the journey back to ourselves and our spirituality.

Most of us have some strange ideas about meditation. We think that to meditate we have to be some shaven-headed monk sitting cross-legged in a monastery far from the maddening crowd. This image might be nice and it just doesn't fit in with the way most Westerners live our lives. For meditation to be an everyday thing, we need to discover the ways we already have meditation in our lives.

For some, it may be playing the piano or listening to music. For others, it may be taking a walk or just sitting and looking out. For others, we may need something more active, like cleaning the stove, washing and polishing the car, refinishing furniture, or even fishing.

Many of us find ways and times to move into a meditative state that heals and grounds us without even letting ourselves know we are doing it. However, our being knows.

Can we ever meditate too much?

Getting Help

*I'm frantic about moving. We have to be out in
the next few days. But no one can help us because
we have to sort through everything before we move
it and then we need to put it where we want it.*

J.

Accepting and receiving help is a fine art practiced by
few and recognized by even fewer.

Often, we have friends standing by ready to help
who would even, perhaps, feel really good about themselves by being helpers, and we just do not give them
that opportunity.

We get frantic about what we have to do and we
work ourselves into a steam and we just have to do it all
by ourselves, for ourselves. (In fact, if we admitted it, we
might even secretly enjoy the steam a bit!)

How sad it is that we do not let those who care
about us and love us have the pleasure of being there for
us and doing things for us that show us their love and
caring.

If they love us, they have to sit by and watch us kill
ourselves, yet do nothing.

**When I think I have to do everything myself, I have
forgotten how to be loved.**

Feelings

Worry is one of the best techniques I have to avoid
my feelings.

ANONYMOUS

Few of us have had really good skill-training in dealing
with our feelings. We learn reading, math, business, and
cooking, but no one seems interested in or capable of
teaching us about feelings. Often, we learn that feelings
are dangerous and, given an inch, they will completely
run amuck and get us in terrible trouble. Feelings, after
all, are not rational and logical. And, safety is in logic
and rationality.

What a sad state of affairs! Would the Creator have
given us feelings if they were all that bad? I doubt it!

Feelings let us know where we are and who we are.
Feelings warn us of danger and let us know when someone is lying to us.

Feelings let us experience happiness and love, and
loneliness and fear. Feelings let us know when we are
doing just fine and when we need to pay attention and
make some changes.

When we avoid our feelings, we avoid ourselves.

Wrongs/Wisdom

A man should never be ashamed to own he has been in the wrong, which is but saying, in other words, that he is wiser today than he was yesterday.

ALEXANDER POPE

How many opportunities do we actually get in a day to show that we are wiser than we were the day before? Not many!

We are so accustomed to barrages of defensiveness when mistakes are discovered that we are almost always startled when people admit they are wrong.

For some people, admitting we are wrong is not enough. They want us to feel bad. To admit we are wrong *and* not feel bad about it and castigate ourselves seems un-American. In fact, some people feel so strongly about the need to suffer when we are wrong that they are willing to beat up on us if we won't do it ourselves.

It certainly would be a lot easier to admit we were in the wrong and use it to become wiser in the long run if someone didn't want that pound of flesh.

We can always start with ourselves and support others admitting their wrongs by doing it ourselves. Wisdom is, after all, its own reward.

Altered Perceptions

Worry and fear can alter our perceptions until we lose all sense of reality, twisting neutral situations into nightmares.

THE COURAGE TO CHANGE

Rarely do we stop and think that some of the processes in which we indulge actually alter our perceptions and distort our reality. Ironically, as we indulge in worry and fear, we even lose the ability to have a perspective on our reality and notice when we are altering it. Because of this lack of perspective, we become even more wedded to our perceptions and try to force ourselves and others into believing the truth of our distorted perceptions. The whole process can be very exhausting.

We need friends we can trust to help us regain our perspective and to stop the downward spiral of worry and fear.

We also need to realize that there are forces in the universe greater than we and that, ultimately, we need to bow to them.

Funny, isn't it, how friends and a power greater than ourselves can neutralize nightmares?

Following Our Hearts

Carefully observe what way your heart draws you, and then choose that way with all your strength.

HASSIDIC SAYING

We hear a lot these days about following our bliss—easier said than done!

It often takes a lot of listening to observe where our hearts draw us. We do not receive much skill-training in our families and schools for this behavior. In fact, we find ourselves being much clearer about what we *should* do, what others *want* us to do, and what we *have* to do, than we are about where our hearts are leading us.

If we find ourselves deficient in the heart-leading area, we may have to start with some baby steps before we leap to what our hearts want us to do with our lives. We can start with small questions, such as . . . what colors feel good on our skin? . . . what foods do we especially like? . . . what kinds of books and music do we truly like to read and listen to?

After we have flexed our muscles a little, then we might stop and ask, whom do we really want to spend our time with? Who are the people who feed our souls? Then, only then, we might be ready to move on to bigger and better things.

Following our hearts may involve some preliminary baby steps and some shedding of old habits.

Commitment

Worry is prayer for what you don't want.
                                    JESSE SPINNLER

Frequently, we have a much clearer idea of what we don't want than what we want. After so many years of focusing upon what we *don't* want, we find it increasingly difficult to focus upon what we *do* want.

One of the terrors of beginning to focus upon what we really do want is fear of commitment. When we venture into the realm of what we want, we are putting ourselves out there, making a commitment to ourselves and taking responsibility for what we want. This commitment behavior is scary stuff! What if we are wrong? What if we make a mistake?

It is much easier to slip and slide around in the foggy, gray area of negativity than to venture forth and take responsibility for our lives. Worry gives us an out.

After all, if I make a commitment to what I do want and take responsibility for it, that's like becoming an adult, isn't it?

Gratitude

Gratitude is the memory of the heart.
LYDIA M. CHILD

A friend of mine talks about having gratitude attacks. I like that. I also like the idea of gratitude being the "memory of the heart."

Our minds, when left to their own tendencies, can conjure up all sorts of horrible ideas, embellish them, dress them in full regal outfits, and construct castles in which they can dwell. Our minds can even convince us that our lives are awful and just too, too difficult.

Fortunately, our hearts tend to run a more even course. When we let our hearts remember, all kinds of wonderful memories come into focus. We remember that there is always the promise of a new day and the sun will rise even if we don't see it. We remember that we will have weather and that the range of weathers feeds the earth. We remember a forgotten smile or kind word when all seemed despair. We remember that we were able to reach out to someone who needed it even when we felt needy.

Gratitude is everything.

Using Others

*I discovered when I quit worrying about my kids,
I had to shift into a whole new phase of my life—
what do I want to do with my life. That was
scary.*

PATTI

We often use others without any awareness whatsoever
that we are doing it. Most of us have a certain disdain
for the very idea of using others and we are sure that we
would never do that in a million years.

How surprised we would be if we let ourselves see
that we not only use people, we mostly tend to use people
who are the nearest and dearest to us . . . our children . . .
our spouses . . . our best friends! They are so convenient
and close at hand. How easy it is to focus on them
and their lives and use that focus as an escape from intimacy with ourselves. As long as we can worry and keep
the focus elsewhere, we do not have to deal with the
scary business of getting on with our lives and letting ourselves be truly vulnerable to those we love.

*Using others does not fit with my self-image . . . soooo
. . . why do I do it?*

Relationships

Being an old maid is like death by drowning—a really delightful sensation after you have ceased struggling.

EDNA FERBER

Fear of being "alone" in our old age has been a great cause of concern and has resulted in lots of frantic mismatches in this world.

I recently discovered a whole new way to look at relationships. What if we did not start out in the womb believing that we should and must find a mate? What if the focus we taught our children was that their purpose in being here was to live their own life, and that some people might do that in conjunction with someone else and others wouldn't? What if each of us accepted the pure and simple mandate of living the life we were given, and paid full attention to that while believing that if the Creator wanted us to do it with a mate, the Creator would find us one and plunk that person right directly in our path with no ifs, ands, or buts?

We wouldn't need to "hunt" for a mate, thus eliminating a lot of false starts. And we wouldn't need to "manage" relationships. There wouldn't even be "old maids" and "bachelors." Life would just be lived.

When we cease struggling with our life as it is, it gets better.

Experts

I'm with the experts. Why worry!

MARY JANE

Sometimes I think the time to start worrying is when I am with the "experts." Usually the "experts" are people who, by definition, know more about myself and my life than I do. This is, indeed, a dangerous situation.

We have all had so much training in turning our lives over to the experts that we have gradually gotten out of touch with our ability to discern what we really need and which people might be able to help us get it. We set ourselves up to be victims by turning our lives over to whoever says they are experts.

I once heard a definition of "expert" that tickled me—"X" is an unknown quantity and a "spurt" is a drip under pressure. Now, really, do we want to turn our lives over to an unknown quantity who is a drip under pressure? Think twice.

How I define "expert" may be a life-and-death matter.

Adversity

A poet in adversity can hardly make verses.

PROVERB

Sometimes, we get in the habit of demanding too much of ourselves. Life is so structured that there will be times of adversity. Adversities in life are not a fluke. They are as much a part of living as happy times, peaceful times, quiet times, and productive times. Life has its cycles, and they are not always up.

Unfortunately, we tend to make hard times more adverse by pretending that we really are not going through a difficult time. When we do not acknowledge times of adversity, we tend to become very demanding of ourselves. We not only deal with the *unusual* things that are happening, we feel that we must accomplish business as usual as well as deal with the immediacy of the particular adversity.

Asking ourselves to carry on normally in the middle of adversity is cruel and unusual punishment.

Relaxation

There are two days in the week about which and
upon which I never worry. Two carefree days,
kept sacredly free from fear and apprehension.
One of these days is Yesterday—and the other day
I do not worry about is Tomorrow.

ROBERT JAMES BURDETTE

If today is the tomorrow I thought about yesterday, and yesterday and tomorrow are the two days of the week about which I need not worry, then I can relax. Relaxing is what I do when I let myself know that I am not in control of the universe. Relaxing is the aftereffect of letting go of my mental chatter, sending the committee that resides in my head on vacation, and letting my mind know the freedom of "now."

Often, we do not let ourselves know how unrelaxed we are until we start to relax. Sometimes, we get headaches when we begin to relax because we have been so tense for so long that the unwinding actually causes pain. When we let ourselves go through that pain, we can begin to know relaxation.

A tense body and a tense mind re-create themselves daily moment by moment.

Expectations

Nothing is so wretched or foolish as to anticipate misfortunes. What madness is it to be expecting evil before it comes.

SENECA

Seneca reminded us that it is madness to expect evil before it comes. However, he did not go so far as to remind us that expectations themselves are a kind of madness. If the old saying that "expectations are premeditated resentments" is true, then our expectations are always putting us in an untenable position.

Often, we are so tied up with our expectations that we actually miss what is. We are so focused upon what isn't or what we think we want that we have no time or energy to respond to what is actually happening in our lives.

Life, as we live it, is not a setup of prescheduled events that have no relationship to one another. Life is an unfolding in which we can participate. What we anticipate may not be nearly as wonderful or as healing as what we get.

I am only disappointed when I think I know what will or should happen.

Our Bodies

Not only can worry be responsible for
susceptibility to disease, it can extinguish energy
and, finally, turn life into barely tolerable misery.

REV. LEE TRUMAN

What wonderful things are these bodies we have! When we stop and think of all the things we do each day *not* to take care of our bodies, it's amazing that we have any health at all. We put ourselves through constant worry and stress with nary a thought about what we are doing to our bodies (of course, we could worry about that, too). We breathe in pollution and carcinogens. We put foods, medicines, tobacco smoke, and drugs and alcohol into our bodies without stopping to think what we are doing to them . . . and, still they carry on.

How long has it been since we stopped, took stock, and listened to what our bodies really need? How often do we let ourselves realize that we have within us the most marvelous mechanisms and processes for healing that exist? How often do we let up from battering our bodies to just say "thanks"?

When we begin to see the wonder of our bodies, we may begin to see the wonder of ourselves.

Control

*I think of true neurotics as people who would
rather hold on to their illusion of control than run
the risk of getting what they want.*

ANNE WILSON SCHAEF

Our need for control is so deep and so subtle that we
sometimes do not even realize that it exists at all. Most
of us do not like to think of ourselves as controlling and
even if we let ourselves catch a glimpse of our controlling tendencies, we quickly say, "Well, it's not *that* bad."

I saw an old hen once with a lot of little chickens.
She was a good mother and clucked and scratched hard
to find food for her babies. She would not let them stray
far from her and she kept a close eye on them. One day,
she was scratching and clucking in the dirt and not
finding much. Still, she kept the babies close. One of
the little chicks wandered just a bit and found a cache
of grain on the ground and happily started pecking
away. When she discovered this little chick had strayed,
she got so involved in making a big fuss and calling it
back that she didn't even notice that that chick had
found the food she had been looking for.

**We tend to believe that if we are in control, we won't
have to deal with surprises. Getting what I want may
involve surprises.**

Fear/Trust

The more I traveled the more I realized that fear makes strangers of people who should be friends.
SHIRLEY MACLAINE

How much of our lives is ruled by fear? Often when we travel we are afraid to reach out to people because of fear, and we filter out connections that could have been friendly.

Trust is an interesting issue. We tend to be very dualistic about trust. We seem to feel that we should be trusting and open and we try to trust everyone, even when they are not trustworthy. In fact, in our arrogance, we demand that untrustworthy people be trustworthy and refuse to see them as they really are. Who they really are is irrelevant to our need to define them and to see ourselves as trustworthy.

Or, we go to the other extreme. We won't trust anybody. Again, we want our definition of everyone to be the one that counts. We approach the trust issue from a self-centered perspective.

There's a third option. It is our responsibility to trust our guts and use our heads and see who can be trusted up close and who needs to be trusted only at a very safe distance. We have that ability. We only need to use it.

Trust is not either/or. I have the ability to discern who can be trusted and who cannot once I am clear.

Worry/Spirituality

Words and phrases about worry:
Worry wart
What if
Worry yourself sick
Worry yourself to death
Don't worry me
Worrying—picking at something—pick at a hole
*   until you have a big one*
Worry beads
Worry stone

CAPTAIN QUEEG

These are not the kinds of images that would make one feel good about oneself, are they? Why is it that when we feel hassled, we indulge in behaviors that ultimately make us feel worse about ourselves? Worrying and the way we think about ourselves when we are worrying feed into a downward spiral and gather momentum during their descent.

Perhaps, if there is anything we have learned about worry by looking at it more carefully, it is that we cannot control it. We cannot will it to go away.

The only thing that really works is the admission that we are powerless over our worrying and there is a power greater than ourselves to whom we can give it.

How often we forget to turn to our spirituality with everyday matters.

Life's Stages

Remember that as a teenager you are in the last
stage of your life when you will be happy to hear
the phone is for you.

FRAN LEBOWITZ

How comforting to remember that life is a process and that there are stages to it. What we rejoice in at one stage—like playing in the mud, for example—would be miserable at another time (especially in a business suit).

Life's stages give us an opportunity to play with our lives. Take the telephone, for example. Almost all teenagers truly believe that the telephone is a necessary extension of themselves. Nothing is so horrible as being without one. Yet, as we grow older we come to dread it.

Life itself is one of the best teachers we have to challenge our illusion of absolutes. Try as we might, we find it impossible to force stagnation upon ourselves. How sad it is when we stubbornly refuse to move through life's stages and try to hold on to those that are no longer relevant for us.

Life's stages challenge our need for absolutes.

Levels of Truth

*When I don't have anything to worry about, I
begin to worry about that.*

WALTER KELLY

You can't keep a good man down, can you? I mean really
. . . let's give credit where credit is due. Some people
are just plain creative in their worry patterns.

One of the most important things in life is to know
when we are good at something and appreciate that
gift. Clearly, Walter Kelly is good at worrying. He has
perfected the knowledge that worrying can take place
at many levels and that if one level is inactive, it is
always possible immediately to switch to another level
and get busy.

Life is sorta like that, isn't it? It occurs on many
levels of truth at the same time. If we are trying to operate on one level of truth and those around us are operating on another, confusion ensues unless we can see and
respect one another's levels of truth. Conflict results
when people who have little awareness of the levels of
truth on an issue demand that others be on their level
of truth.

**Life exists on many levels. Just because someone is
not on my level does not mean that one of us is wrong.**

Faith and Doubt

*Faith and doubt both are needed—not as
antagonists, but working side by side—to take us
around the unknown curve.*

LILLIAN SMITH

Eric Erickson, the well-known German psychologist
who immigrated to the U.S., delineated what he called
the psycho-social stages of growth. In each stage, he
named two seemingly opposing characteristics that,
when balanced, resulted in what he called a "virtue."
For example, he named the two characteristics of the
first stage of life—basic trust and basic mistrust. As they
work together and balance each other, the virtue that is
developed is hope.

In our dualistic thinking, we tend to see one as
good and one as bad. Not so. In order to grow and
thrive, we need to develop a basic trust for that which
can be trusted and a mistrust for that which cannot be
trusted. Otherwise, hope is not possible.

Faith and doubt are like that. My faith is essential
to my being and lets me know where I am in time and
space. My doubt is the only pill I have for my gullibility.
Together they equip me for the unknown.

Life is, after all, a continuous "unknown curve."

Relationships

Whoever gossips to you will gossip about you.
SPANISH PROVERB

Why are we so arrogant as to be sure the people we care about will not treat us as we have seen them treat others in their lives?

Often, in our relationships, we get lulled into believing that "this one is different": "I have seen the person I love treat their previous partner badly but that person would never do that to me because she/he loves me." Wrong!

Wanting to believe that "this is different" is part of stubborn gullibility. We want to believe that our relationship is different and that people are "healed" by our loving them. Beware! Beware of our own gullibility.

Unless that person has done some real work on themselves, has made some basic changes, and has learned some tools for living under stress, the same old behaviors will blossom. We can't control this blossoming. We can, however, do something about our surprise when it happens.

A tiger can't change its stripes (without a lot of work!).

Messes

*I have no time for people who do what they want
to do and then snuff it, leaving everything they
ought to have done to those of us who are left.*

Some of us go through life looking straight ahead and
leaving a trail of destruction in our wake. We have little
awareness of the clutter behind us.

Maybe a big part of growing up is doing what we
want to do, while, at the same time, taking responsibility for our messes. Both are possible.

I know there have been times when I just wanted
to take other people's messes and dump them on their
front doorstep. Yet, I need to take some responsibility
for letting them pile up on me. If I had practiced shoveling them out on a daily basis, I wouldn't have the
garbage heap. Instead, if I start with shoveling mine out
on a daily basis, I wouldn't have *my* garbage heap either.

Frankly, I never signed up to be a sanitation worker.

Being in the Given

We are born to live on the given. Not the taken.

BERT WHITE

Did you ever go to the refrigerator and the cupboards after unexpected company has just arrived, only to discover that they both look quite bare . . . and then go on to prepare a gourmet meal? Or, did you ever have an appliance break down on the weekend with nary a repair person in sight, and then discover that you could fix it yourself with spare parts? You felt good about yourself, didn't you?

Life is sometimes like the refrigerator that looks empty. We have grown so accustomed to taking and expecting that more is better that we have come to neglect the resources that are our givens.

For example, we may have good health, or a talent for keeping track of leftovers and knowing how to make unusual combinations. We may have energy to burn when everyone else has collapsed in a heap, or we may be able to listen to a whole group of people brainstorming and pull together the threads into an organizational tapestry.

Whatever our givens, when we recognize and value them, our lives seem easier.

I'll never be able to take what I need to live this life. It has been given.

Having Nothing to Do

Sometimes I just worry when there's nothing else to do.

BETTY

Now, Betty is a person who believes in proverbs—"An idle mind is the devil's workshop." It's important to keep busy. Remember when we were kids and we discovered that if we *looked* busy in school (regardless of what we were doing!) we didn't get in trouble? Isn't it interesting how those childhood learnings carry over into adulthood?

Indeed, if we are honest about it, we're a little afraid of nothing to do. If we don't have anything to do, it must mean that we are not important . . . if we don't have anything to do, those feelings and memories that we have been trying so hard to keep down for all these years might just erupt . . . if we don't have anything to do, someone might think we are lazy. Thank goodness for worry. Worry can fill in the gaps!

Having nothing to do may be a gift, not an attack.

Inevitables

I hate housework! You make the beds, you do the dishes—and six months later you have to start all over again.

JOAN RIVERS

Why is it when death and taxes are listed as the "inevitables" that housework isn't included? I love the quote by Quentin Crisp, "There was no need to do any housework at all. After the first four years the dirt doesn't get any worse."

Maybe it's time to sit down and take a look at the inevitables. In fact, maybe life is basically made up of inevitables and it is not they that are the problem but what we do with them. It may be our refusal to accept the inevitables that gives us headaches, bloody scalps, and sore necks, and not the inevitables themselves.

For example, can we control what our children do with their lives? . . . Probably not. Can we control what other people think about us? . . . Probably not. Can we keep disasters from happening? . . . Probably not. Can we accept what we can't control? Probably.

Maybe the meaning of life is learning to live creatively with the inevitables.

Choices

*There are some questions you can ask that add
fuel to the worry fire.*

CHUCK

Remember those times when we have been frantically
worried about someone we love? It's surprising to realize
that even during times of extreme distress, we have
choices.

We may choose to feed our distress by asking,
"What if this happens?"—"What if that happens?" and
in so doing feed our anxiety and our fears. The payoffs,
of course, to feeding our distress are humongous shots of
adrenaline and lots of good crisis energy to feed on.

We can also choose to ask other questions, like,
"What would I be doing right now if I weren't feeding
my disaster orientation?" and maybe we can even go
and do whatever it is . . . or we can ask ourselves, "What
feelings am I avoiding by feeding this crisis?" and deal
with the feelings.

**It's important to remember that I am in charge of the
questions I ask myself. "What ifs" may not be the best
choice.**

Look on the Bright Side

*E tutaki ana nga kapua o te rangi, kei runga te
Mangoroa e kopae pu ana.*

The clouds in the sky close over, but above
them spreads the Milky Way.

MAORI PROVERB

I doubt any of us can truthfully claim to have never had
a sunny day or a good moment in our lives!

All my life, I have been accused of being an optimist. Strange, the label has frequently been accompanied
with a slight tinge of negativism. Yet, when we think of
optimism, we usually think of it as the opposite of negativism and also see it as unrealistic and starry-eyed. That
view of optimism misses the point completely.

Optimism is a memory exercise. Optimism is remembering our experience that the stars of the Milky
Way are just beyond the clouds. Optimism is remembering that last year's disaster proved to be one of our major learning experiences. Optimism is remembering that
when we didn't get what we thought we wanted, what
we eventually got was even better.

*Remember, just as the clouds evaporate in the sun,
negativism has a difficult time withstanding optimism.*

Worry Boxes

I don't worry about anything anymore. People call me because they're worried, and I listen to them three hours a day. That's put a stop to my worrying. And besides, every worry I've ever had has happened. I worried about being fired, and that's happened eighteen times.

SALLY JESSY RAPHAEL

On one side, there are those dedicated worriers who think that worrying about something will prevent its happening, and on the other side there are those who believe that if we worry about something, we "draw energy" to it and bring it about. Heavens! What's a body to do with our spare time, anyway?

They say that one of the best forms of birth control is to lend your friends your children for a while. Sally Jessy Raphael seems to have "cured" herself of worry by surrounding herself with "worriers" for three hours a day. Maybe this approach worked for her, yet it seems much like getting bitten by snakes in order to get over your fear of snakes. There must be a gentler, softer way!

Perhaps the issue is the focus on worry. Maybe there's something we would rather be doing with our time.

How about making a "worry box"? Write your worries down, put them in the box, and let them go. (It's always fun to clean the box out a year later!)

Plunging In

*Life is an unfoldment, and the further we travel
the more truth we comprehend. To understand the
things that are at our door is the best preparation
for understanding those that lie beyond.*

HYPATIA

Imagine! Hypatia knew these truths nearly two thousand years ago. Where did we unlearn the truth that life is an unfoldment and that we can only learn its truths as we live them? Pondering is no substitute for experience. Sometimes we are so busy pondering that we rob ourselves of experience. Then, when the next experience comes, we are not prepared for it because we have robbed ourselves of the experiences at hand.

The most important learnings of life cannot be done abstractly. Abstractions do not prepare us. They distract us.

Plunging into life may look like plunging into an icy bath. At least when we jump into that pool we *experience* that it's cold.

Plunging in may be the only sure way of learning that we never want to do that *again*.

Buzz

What is the relationship between worry and adrenaline?

ANONYMOUS

Can it be that worry is our cover-up for our basic and well-loved adrenaline addiction? Adrenaline is one of our easiest and most convenient "fixes." We never have to carry extra substances or equipment like needles or bottles. We can give ourselves a shot of adrenaline at a second's notice and we can have a dependable "high."

Worry is one of our favorite "triggers" for an adrenaline "high." In fact, worriers who become addicted to adrenaline often begin to find "normal" day-to-day life rather boring.

I remember a friend who was recovering from alcoholism. After several years of recovery, she said to me, "You know, I'm feeling rather quiet and peaceful. Nothing much is happening. Life is just going along. Do you think that this is what 'normal' people call 'happy'?" . . . Maybe.

When we have to create a crisis to feel happy and alive, we'd better step back and take a serious look at ourselves.

Sorrow

Sorrow is soon enough when it comes.

PROVERB

Sorrow is part of life. It is not "abnormal" nor is it a "punishment from the gods." Coping with sorrow is one of the learning experiences we have in this life. We cannot get better at coping with it through practicing ahead of time. And we will rarely know how we are going to deal with it until it happens.

Hopefully, our life experiences, our willingness to deal with them as they unfold, and our link with our spirituality will prove to be all we need when sorrow comes.

Sometimes, we try to rush sorrow by wishing it would happen when we feel prepared for it. Or we practice, like "pre-grieving" the death of a parent before the inevitable happens. Yet, we can never truly know how we will deal with any event until it happens. Life's just like that.

Sorrow is meant to be felt—not avoided.

Self-Abuse/Neglect

Worriers do not know that they abuse and neglect themselves every day.

SUE WHITAKER

Do we ever stop and notice the little ways we neglect and abuse ourselves every day? For example, did you ever notice that not going to the bathroom when you have to go is neglect and abuse? Our bodies get tired for a reason. Our bodies get sick for a reason. Ignoring what our bodies are telling us is a form of abuse and neglect.

Worrying is stressful. Worrying affects the body in the same way as anxiety—both add numbers to our blood pressure.

Most worriers would not think of themselves as neglecters and abusers. Yet, they are. Worrying is a lonely place. If we are quiet about it, we become isolated. If we talk on and on about it, we drive others away and . . . we become isolated. Isolating ourselves from the support of others is abusive.

Self-abuse and neglect are something I can do something about and **I have to be aware of them before I can start changing.**

Differences

To be alone is to be different; to be different is to be alone.

SUZANNE GORDON

That's it! Suzanne Gordon has just verbalized one of our greatest fears—BEING ALONE!

We live in a culture that has a terror of aloneness. Aloneness is viewed as a failure. Aloneness is proof positive that we are not acceptable. Aloneness is unacceptable and deplorable . and . . . to be avoided at all costs.

If each of us is a different, unique creation (as we are), and to be different is to be alone, and to be alone is a fate worse than death, no wonder we meet so few people who are who they really are.

If the universe is a huge puzzle and each of us is a piece of that puzzle, when we refuse to be who we are and try to be someone else, there is a hole in the universe. It seems we have reached a time when there are a lot of holes in the universe.

If I refuse to be who I am, I contribute a hole, not a puzzle piece, to the universe.

Helplessness

Worrying is being informed. Being informed is worrying and talking about it. I watched Desert Storm twenty-four hours a day and quoted the commentators. That's being informed and caring.

BETH

One of the good things about the world we live in today is that if we are informed, we can pick up on endless possibilities for worry. In fact, with the information explosion, we have developed an emerging need for worry specialists. With so much going on in our homes, the cities, our country, and the world, no one, even an accomplished worrier, can keep up with it all.

We have come to believe that being informed, worrying, and talking about whatever is going on around us is a form of caring. Maybe this information → worry → talking → caring → information loop isn't the answer. Maybe we need to confront our feelings of helplessness. We are truly powerless over so much of what happens around us. When we can confront our feelings of powerlessness we are on the way to spirituality.

Experiencing my feelings of helplessness may be the door I have been looking for into my spirituality.

Internal Revolts

PERSONALIZED SERENITY PRAYER

God grant me
the serenity to accept the ones I cannot change,
the courage to change the one I can,
and the wisdom to know it's me.

ANONYMOUS

The only person I can change is myself. Most of us receive this wisdom with a knowing nod of the head. We glaze our eyes and display a wise, knowing smile. Of course, everyone knows that it is not really possible to change anyone else.

Then, something strange begins to happen .. a voice within our heads begins to SCREAM—I DON'T BELIEVE THAT GARBAGE FOR A MINUTE. Our guts begin to twist and lurch and the very fibers of our being move into violent revolt!

This battle is one of those interesting situations where our wisdom and our behavior collide. Our rational minds know the wisdom in the knowledge that the only person we can change is ourselves, and our inner beings scream out, "We'll see!"

When we go into internal revolts, it's good to wait until the screaming stops before we try to act.

Anticipation

Nothing is so good as it seems beforehand.
GEORGE ELIOT

Anticipation is a wonderful toy! We can take it out and play with it or secretly and tenderly hold it close to our heart so no one can see.

Taste buds are great at anticipation. We start salivating as the smell of roasted garlic wafts in from the kitchen heralding a favorite meal. What fun to enjoy that saliva!

Our bodies can remember the comfort of snuggling up next to the person we love, and when we have been away we can tingle with anticipation of that known comfort.

The problem is not with the anticipation. Anticipation is one of the toys the Creator has given us to play with in life.

Our problems come when we try to superimpose our fantasies of anticipation on the actual moment. When we try to force our anticipations upon the moment, we miss the moment. The moment may be nothing like we imagined. And, the moment may contain a whole new array of surprises.

Why rob ourselves of the anticipation and the moment. We can have both!

Taking Responsibility

Worrying is not an option. It is a responsibility.

NAN

Taking responsibility for our own lives is such an unusual and tricky issue these days. We seem to be very confused about the concept of responsibility. Unfortunately, we have come to equate responsibility with blame and none of us wants to be *blamed* for anything.

Yet, responsibility does not really mean blame. Healthy responsibility-taking is more like ownership—owning the choices we have made and being willing to deal with the consequences.

The temptation is to try to find something or someone outside ourselves that is responsible for our choices. We cast about for someone to *blame* for our decisions and our lives. In so doing, we give away our power. We disenfranchise ourselves from our lives and become impotent victims.

The other side of the coin is when, like Nan, we take on the responsibility for everything, which is also a power giveaway.

Taking responsibility for our lives is a tricky business and we'd better learn how to do it or we won't have our lives.

Respectability

*Now that I'm over sixty, I'm veering toward
respectability.*

SHELLEY WINTERS

Respectability is wasted on the young! Luckily, they
don't have much use for it, so this particular waste is not
much of a problem.

When we think of respectability, we usually focus
on how others see us and on our attempts to control
others' responses to who we are . . . again, what a waste.

Respectability goes much deeper than either of
these two issues. When we get right down to it, the core
issue of respectability is respecting ourselves.

Do we respect the decisions we make? Do we behave in a way that is congruent to our deepest values?
When we don't behave in a way we wish we had, are we
ready to show ourselves the compassion of caring?

Respectability is a treasure and it is possible at any age.

Illusion of Control

Trying to figure out and control my world and my feelings—that's all worry really is. It's wonderful to have another option now.

PAUL

Why do we spend so much time and energy trying to figure everything out? Listen to any conversation . . . in an airport, a restaurant, a bar, at home! Everyone is trying to get to the "why." What do we gain from our interpretation of the "why"? Does having a grasp on the "why"—any "why"—help feed our illusion of control? Ah ha! That's it! Back to this sneaky little illusion of control.

Figuring out and trying to control—"that's all worry really is." Nice to have worry broken down to its component parts. Now maybe we can control it.

My illusion of control is very cunning. I can disguise it in many costumes and it's still control.

Perspective

This too shall pass.

ABRAHAM LINCOLN

What a comforting phrase, "This too shall pass."

Often, when we are in the middle of a crisis or a fear, all thinking and awareness stop. Our entire beings are focused upon *coping*. Stepping out of our situation and reflecting upon it are beyond the realm of possibility. We become so enmeshed in the problem that the problem becomes our lives. Who needs to eat, sleep, relax, or exercise when they have "the problem"?

These times of crisis are the very times when we need people in our lives who can give us perspective. These are the times when we need to reach out for the comfort of someone who can honestly say, "This too shall pass."

When I'm tied up in self-perpetuating knots, using the phone lines often can help me get untied.

Getting Off Our Parents' Backs

I don't worry—my mother worries for me.

ADONA

At last, we have found the true definition of motherhood. A good mother is one who not only relieves her children of worrying, she makes sure that the worry corner is covered!

Many of us spend so much of our life defining and focusing on the limitations of our parents. Now here's another failure we can add to our list. . . . Our mothers have just not perfected their worry to the point where we can be completely free of worrying for ourselves. When will they ever shape up?!

Of course, we have to admit that if our parents were to really shape up, they might rob us of one of our favorite areas of worry—our relationship with them.

Part of growing up is learning to let our parents be. Indeed, it is learning to let everyone be.

When my favorite distractions no longer work, I have to deal with myself.

Focusing Ourselves

*I cannot know what the future will bring. My best
hope is every bit as likely to occur as my worst
fear, so I have no reason to give more weight to
my negative assumptions. All I can do is to make
the most of this day.*

THE COURAGE TO CHANGE

Today is today. It is a gift from the Creator and it is really
more limited by me than I am by it.

Often, we believe it is too simple to say that we do
not know what tomorrow will bring. We truly don't.
However, we can ruin tomorrow's surprises if we focus
solely on the negative possibilities. A negative focus
can result in our entirely missing the possibilities placed
in our path. Indeed, we become so paralyzed by our
negative focus that we will not even let ourselves wander into places where something good might happen.

**When I'd rather ruin my day than take the risk of my
"best hope" occurring, I'm stuck in the negative. I'd
better call a spiritual tow truck.**

Using Our Minds

I don't believe all worry is bad. Do you? I think of worry as a kind of preparation or planning. It can be helpful.

BETSY MARTIN

Remember that last hot fudge sundae? It's not really *that* bad for me! Just one won't hurt. Remember the last excuse we used not to exercise? I don't have time. I'll start tomorrow.

Remember the excuse we used not to apologize for something we had done which we knew wasn't good? It wasn't really my fault. Probably no one noticed anyway.

Our minds are such wonderful mechanisms. They can take any thought or behavior and turn it into whatever we want it to be. Frequently, however, the only people we really fool are ourselves.

Using our minds is great. Unfortunately, anything that can be used can be misused.

Bad Moods

*Borrow trouble for yourself, if that's your nature,
but don't lend it to your neighbors.*

RUDYARD KIPLING

Did you ever think that worry is like an infectious, contagious disease? No one is immune and there is no known vaccination.

Rarely do we realize how much our moods affect those around us. Even if the people in our lives have good boundaries and are sane enough not to get all enmeshed in our moods, at the very best, we are no fun to be around when we persist in worry and gloom and doom.

It's okay to be in a bad mood. All of us are in a bad mood sometimes. No one can be "up" all the time. We don't have to go around like Pollyanna, cheering everyone up. However, when we are in a bad mood, it's important to admit it, own the mood. Then we can warn those close to us that this is *our* mood and we are working with it. This mood really doesn't have anything to do with them. This kind of "warning device" gives others a chance to back off gracefully and gives us a chance to have the time we need to work with ourselves. This approach is not only very efficient, it's very sane.

My bad moods are for me to work with, not for others to deal with.

Patience

When I begin to worry about whether this relationship will last or not, I usually do something to break it up. I can't stand the tension.

SUE

Why is it that taking the risk of getting what we want seems to be loaded with too much tension to bear? We want our relationships to last and we just can't stand the tension of seeing whether they will last or not. We would rather know what we are dealing with and then we will deal with it.

The anxiety and stress of those suspended times when nothing is agreed upon or completely nailed down just seem too much to bear, don't they? We get to a point where we would rather destroy the possibility than wait for the slow, gradual evolution of a relationship.

Where was it that we were taught that relationships were a task to be accomplished? Where did we get the idea that once a relationship is "nailed down," we can ignore it and get on to bigger and better things?

Our need to know may destroy the process of knowing.

Simple Joys

We have a tendency to obscure the forest of simple joys with the trees of problems.

CHRISTIANE COLLANGE

This might be a good day to catalogue the simple joys that surround us today. Sometimes, we so want to fill our lives with what we consider complex pleasures— like money, possessions, more prestigious friends—that we forget to stop and notice the simple joys that are with us day to day.

For example, each day brings the assurance of a new day. Yesterday may have been a dog and one thing is certain, it could not go on forever. Tomorrow will be a new day. Hopefully, something we learned yesterday will have the potential of making today different.

We have the miraculous power of our bodies to heal. When we cut our finger, or scratch a leg, or get a summer cold, our bodies have a wisdom of healing that transcends our ability to "think it through."

We have weather. Regardless of what the day brings, we can rest assured that we will have weather.

Perhaps one of the reasons I sometimes believe there's nothing I can count on is because I have tried to rely on the wrong things.

Telephones/Spontaneity

My son called me the other day at work. He never calls me at work so my first response was—"Is something wrong?" "No," he said, "I just wanted to talk to you." Then my mind started—"What does he want? Does he need money?" I had trouble just enjoying the call.

PATTI

Phone calls! Phone calls at work! Phone calls late at night or early in the morning! Who invented the telephone, anyway? Shouldn't our children and our friends know that they should only call when we are expecting them to call? There should be a free appointment-screening service included in every telephone hook-up that screens calls and then sets up appointments for calling so that we won't have to deal with unexpected calls, especially from our children. Don't you think so?

We have become afraid of spontaneity. The surprise, even when it is a good one, is almost too much to bear at times, or so it seems, anyway.

Can you believe it? Sometimes, someone important to us just wants to gab with us!

Guidance

I don't think the events of my life are preordained,
but they are definitely guided. I hope they're
guided because I'd have a [heck] of a time trying to
figure it out all by myself!

JOAN BAEZ

Perhaps we have stepped upon the path to wisdom when we begin to see the guidance in our lives. I am one of those persons who just hates to talk with people on airplanes. Usually, when I get on a plane, I am tired and I just want to settle in for a few hours of vegetation. Yet, there have been times when I have just opened to the urge to talk with the person sitting next to me and I have discovered a lifelong friend.

Or, there are those times when everything just seems too much and my whole being is overwhelmed. I'm brought to my knees and I just can't seem to manage it all anymore. I surrender! And then, something else clicks in and takes over. New possibilities appear as if by magic.

I will only recognize the guidance in my life if I am willing to be guided.

Changes

But Jesus, when you don't have any money, the problem is food. When you have money it's sex. When you have both, it's health, you worry about getting ruptured or something. If everything is simply jake then you're frightened of death.

J. P. DONLEAVY

"It's just too good to be true." Remember that old saying? What do we mean, "Too good to be true"? Why do we get so afraid if things are good? It's all right for everything to be fine. It's all right for things to be "simply jake."

We seem not to realize that life is a series of changes, and change applies to all of life. We have focused on our awareness that when things are good, they will change. Of course they will. Change is the nature of life.

What we seem to have forgotten is that when things are bad, they will change, too. Change *is* the nature of life.

It's really not possible to hold on to the good or the bad. They both will change.

Being Human/Being Divine

It's only our fear and lack of faith that cause us to need to be in what we think is control. Yet, self-surrender and letting go in loving trust draw out what is most human in each and every one of us, and, therefore, most divine.

BERT WHITE

My most human is also my most divine. How difficult it is to accept the fact that we are human! Somewhere along the line, we hit upon the idea that our being human was not enough. To be human is too base, too uninteresting. We adopted the idea that we wanted to be supra-human. We wanted to be divine.

How odd to think that the road to our divinity might just unfold through our humanness. We were, after all, created as humans. Our task, then, it would seem, is to be as fully human as possible.

What does it mean to be fully human? It means to honor who we are as human beings. We have feelings. Feelings are not failures. Feelings can be our doors into our divine. We make mistakes. Mistakes are not failures. Mistakes can be our doors into our divine. We get confused and don't know what to do next. Our confusion can cause us to stop and wait, which may be just what we need to do.

Being human isn't an attack on my being. Being human is my being.

Lying

If you lied to me, I would never forgive you. If I lied to you and you caught me, I would never forgive you.

ANONYMOUS

We have become so jaded about lying that sometimes we forget how violent it is. Lying is one of the most violent acts a human being can impose upon another. Honesty can hurt at times, and it is never violent. Lying is always violent. How many friendships have been destroyed by lying?!

One of the ways we protect ourselves from the confrontation of our lying is the incipient threat voiced in saying, "If you ever caught me, I would never forgive you." We try to set up our world so we won't be confronted with our behavior. What a loss!

When friendship demands that I cannot notice what you are doing, it has ceased to be friendship. Friendship can be ruptured by lies and it is always destroyed when it demands ignoring those lies.

Only our real friends can lovingly reflect to us what we have said and done. We all need real friends.

Panic

We experience moments absolutely free from
worry. These brief respites are called panic.
CULLEN HIGHTOWER

Finally! We have sat with this worry issue long enough
that we have found a really positive side to worry!
Worry wards off panic. What a relief!

Panic is completely out of control. Panic can force
us into action, and releases those feelings we have so
desperately wanted to keep at bay. Panic involves the
body on all levels and simply cannot be ignored. Panic
pushes us to new levels of knowing and may even un-
cover those old issues we didn't even know were there.
Panic requires something of us. Panic demands something of us. We cannot ignore panic.

Thank goodness for worry!

Teasing

Fear not a jest. If one throws salt at thee thou wilt receive no harm unless thou hast sore places.

LATIN PROVERB

Teasing has become a tense issue with so many of us. In dysfunctional families, teasing is often used to abuse or put down. So many people in today's society have never had an opportunity to experience teasing as loving.

Yet, teasing can be very loving. In fact, many people only tease those they love and teasing is a loving form of intimacy. Teasing can be a way of saying, "I see this in you and I love you for it."

When we love unconditionally, we see all of a person and we take all of a person into our being. One way to take another person into our most intimate self is to tease them.

If we are being teased lovingly, and the teasing feels like salt on a sore place, the issue may not be the teasing. We may need an opportunity to look at and attend to our "sore places."

Loving teasing is being loved.

Poison

*If you could package it [worry] it would be like
poison in a bottle. It gets into your bloodstream
and you can't shake it.*

CORINNE

Today might be a good day to look at our regular regime
of self-inflicted poisons.

Some people are poisonous for us to be around. Some
people send little poison-tipped acupuncture needles into
our body and our being every time we go near them. We
can't control what they are sending our way, yet we do
have some say in how much time we spend around them.
We can learn to walk away.

However, the majority of poison that gets into
our bloodstream probably has more to do with us and
what we do to ourselves than it has to do with other
people. Take resentment, for example. We have fash-
ioned little time-released capsules of resentment that
let just enough poison out into our bloodstream to keep
us unhappy and confused over long periods of time.

Or, take the disappointment poison, which is not
time-released. It can linger, unnoticed for years, waiting
for just the right catalyst to produce the desired toxic
reaction.

**There's no antidote for our internal poisons except the
willingness to let go, forgive, and move on.**

Getting There by Being There

Before, I knew where I was going but not how to get there. And now, I know how to get there; I just don't know where I'm going.

TAYLOR

We often get hooked by thinking we know where we are going. It is so seductive to have a good destination clearly in mind, even if we haven't a clue what the steps are along the way. We begin to think that only the end point is important. Religions have often focused upon the ultimate end, trying to be like the leader who founded a religion while losing sight of all the processes that he/she went through to become the leader.

Ironically, if we know how to get there, where we're going doesn't really matter that much.

When I just put one foot in front of the other in life, I get there. The beauty is, I don't have to know where "there" is!

Do Something!

Worry makes for a hard pillow. When
something's troubling you, before going to sleep,
jot down three things you can do the next day to
help solve the problem.

LIFE'S LITTLE INSTRUCTION CALENDAR,
VOLUME II

We have often heard that we should never go to bed with our anger (brrrr, what a ghastly idea!). Sleeping with worry under our head sounds even worse. One can envision those hard little blocks of wood the samurai used for pillows in old movies.

Perhaps it would be good to have a "God Box" beside our bed. (When I first heard of a God Box, I gritted my teeth ... and ... when nothing else worked, decided to try it.)

Before going to sleep, just write down each worry on a slip of paper and stick it into your God Box.

Sounds "techniquey," doesn't it?

I'll do anything for a good night's sleep!

Often, it's taking the action that's the important thing, regardless of what the action is.

Tackling "Old Stuff"

*Anxiety is love's greatest killer. It makes others
feel as you might when a drowning man holds on
to you. You want to save him, but you know he
will strangle you with his panic.*

ANAÏS NIN

We worry out of love and we strangle out of love.
What's wrong with this picture?

Often, we forget to remember that our anxiety is
ours. Regardless of what the other person does, our feelings of anxiety are ours alone.

When we have feelings of anxiety in a relationship,
instead of clutching the object of our anxiety more
tightly, we have another option. We can back off!

We can back off, go into ourselves, and let ourselves see what is being triggered by this relationship.
Most times, the strong feeling of anxiety has little or
nothing to do with the situation at hand. The feeling of
anxiety may be a door to work through some old issues
that are ready to be finished.

**Our feelings take us where our brains never could and
can lead us to where we need to be.**

Our Kids (and Ourselves)

*I worried about how I damaged my kids—
everything I had ever regretted. When I got
completely sick of it, it caused me to shift.*

BETTY

None of us has ever known a parent or been a parent who hasn't damaged our kids at one time or another. The whole concept of parents who don't damage their kids is out of the realm of possibility. We are, after all, human, and they are, after all, human. In reality, these human situations are fraught with dangers, and most of us are learning as we go.

We owe it to ourselves and our kids to let it go. Nothing we can give them will be more valuable than the model of admitting our faults and mistakes, forgiving ourselves, making amends to them for what we have done and not done, and presenting them with a more mature and complete adult to relate with than we ever could have when they were little.

In raising kids, we did the best we knew how. In relating to those kids as adults, we continue to have new opportunities.

Sneaky Thoughts That Snake Around

That was a snake that would lay eggs in my brain.
FAITH SULLIVAN,
THE CAPE ANN (1966)

Our brains are fertile nests for snake eggs. The crooks and crevices offer endless opportunities for dark, moist incubators. Some people have said, "My mind is a dangerous neighborhood. I never should go in there alone."

Often, we underestimate the creativity of our brains. We forget that our brains can turn an innocent idea into a snake that can lay eggs. And, like the brown snake of the South Pacific, these thoughts can do it alone. They don't even need another like thought with which to mate.

It's strange, when we open ourselves to these snakelike thoughts, we often look for other people who have sneaky snakes that will reinforce our insanity.

We all feel insane sometimes. We have a choice as to whether we reinforce that insanity or not.

Creativity

*I like to worry every angle of an issue. It's
important not to leave anything out.*

NANCY

One of the saddest experiences in life is not taking our
creativity seriously. We all have gifts, and a big part of
growing up is learning to appreciate our gifts and take
them seriously.

For example, how many people are really *good* at
worrying every angle of an issue? Most of us pedestrian
types of worriers get stuck on one angle and we worry it
to death. But a real creative worrier can generate an infinite number of angles to an issue to worry about. Now,
that's skill!

The rest of us probably leave all kinds of things
out ... but not a creative worrier. A creative worrier
can even make up angles to an issue that don't exist or
haven't been discovered yet ... and then ... he/she
can build on those newly created angles to evolve a
whole new superstructure of worry angles.

**A creative worrier can make a geodesic dome look like
a square. Hooray for creativity—wherever it's found!**

Living in Process

All in due time.

PROVERB

Now isn't this silly that we have made up a proverb that tells us to do what we have no power of not doing anyway?!

Of course, we can spend a great deal of our time and energy trying not to take things as they come or trying to make things come on our time, and all we achieve is frustrated psyches.

When we live our lives as a process, we begin to understand that all life is a process and we have but to participate in it. We don't need to try to control life and life isn't trying to control us. We can participate with one another.

When we take things as they come, we understand that we do not always understand and that understanding often comes while we are participating or after our participation. It is clear that our need to know often keeps us from taking the steps that will lead us to knowing.

God's time—not ours.

Organization

*I have tried to systematize my worry—I have over
a hundred major categories and subcategories.*

LOUISE

Why is it that we have come to believe that organization is the door to control? We long to get our lives organized. We feel so scattered and "out of control." We
are sure that if we could just insert some structure into
our lives, everything would be okay.

The true question is—whose organization? What if
our lives are already organized and we just have not
reached a place inside ourselves where we can appre-
hend the organization? What if we are so busy trying to
impose our simplistic organization that we are unable to
see that there might be a much grander setup in which
we can participate? What if we haven't taken the time
to stop and listen for long enough to hear what life is
saying to us? What if we are using worry to keep the
"noise level" just high enough so we can't hear?

Just asking!

Perhaps we are more organized than we thought.

Advice

The best advice on the art of being happy is about as easy to follow as advice to be well when one is sick.

ANNE SOPHIE SWETCHINE

Want to waste your words? Give advice!

Advice is tricky. We usually ask for it when we have absolutely no intention of using it at all. And, we give it when we are probably the people most in need of hearing what we are saying.

Perhaps advice is really designed to serve a social function. The giving and receiving of advice gives us an illusion of intimacy and closeness. After all, when we ask for advice, isn't that an indirect way of saying to a person, "I value you. I value your wisdom. I care about you," even if we don't intend to follow it. In fact, maybe asking for advice does say all those nice things and at the same time gives us an opportunity to run from the unbearable intimacy it opens up.

And, when we give advice, are we really saying, "I care about you. I want to be able to be the one who says the really helpful clue you need. I want to be indispensable in your life"? When all we need to say is, "I'm sure you know yourself."

Advice-giving and -taking just seems too complex to fool with, doesn't it?

Worry Is Not Planning

The worry habit is often defined as planning.
People are convinced they are doing the right
thing; and besides, they can't stop because, like
freckles, there's no way to scrub worries out of
one's life. They constantly buzz and flit from one
gloomy worry to another, like bees around a hive.

SUE WHITAKER

How easy it is to "con" ourselves into believing that we are not worrying . . . we are just planning.

Take the issue of what to wear, for example . . . we stew and fuss over what we should wear to an important event. We want to figure out what others will be wearing because we want to "fit in." And, yet, we are horrified at the thought that we might turn up with the same outfit as someone else. We want to "stand out" and "make a statement," but we don't want to be seen as outlandish. We hassle. We despair. We obsess. We settle on something and then reject it. We torment ourselves and others. What if the weather changes? What if nothing will really work?

It never occurs to us that we are worrying. It never occurs to us that we can have some options and then trust what "feels" right when the time comes.

When we try to fool ourselves about worrying, we are probably conning ourselves about other things, too.

Negative Thinking/Hope/Faith

How disappointment tracks the steps of hope.
LETITIA E. LANDON

I find it interesting that so many of our well-known quotations are rooted in negative thinking. Our lives are so permeated and controlled by negative thinking that when people are truly positive or hopeful they have come to be seen as unrealistic and naive. Yet, in truth, the real difference is only in what our minds do with the same information.

Let's take hope, for example. When our minds narrow down the things we hope for to one or even two possibilities, we are setting ourselves up for disappointment. We are narrowing the possibility of what we want, and we are increasing the odds against something good happening a thousandfold.

When hope, however, is a faith that everything will turn out all right and we trust that some of those possibilities may even be beyond our grasp at the moment, we have developed a hope undergirded by faith. And, this powerful marriage of hope and faith leaves little room for disappointment.

Hope is great. And *hope supported by faith creates an unbeatable duo.*

Solutions

*Not that these [health and work] aren't
worthwhile concerns. When I'm sober, I can have
them and easily let go. When I'm worried, these
same concerns take on a flavor of fear, control,
and trusting. When I'm connected to my Higher
Power, I can have these concerns and know that
they'll work out in God's time and God's way.
When I'm worried, I want them to work out and I
want to know how and I just don't see how. . . .*

JIM

How difficult it is sometimes to see that "we" are the problem. Our being the problem doesn't mean that we are bad, or that we have done something wrong. Our problem is not centered in who we are. We can make problems for ourselves by the way we choose to approach those problems.

We all have concerns. Health and work are concerns that seem to be part of living in this culture. The issue is: Where do we go from here? If we notice our concerns, think about them, and then rest in the knowledge that we may not have all the information we need and that they *will* work out, we can let them go. When we try to reach a solution before we *know* what our concern really is, we're already in trouble.

Solutions are discovered—not thought out.

Understanding

*If you understand, things are just as they are; if
you do not understand, things are just as they are.*
ZEN PROVERB

How much emphasis we have put on "understanding"!
We have felt confused and bewildered and we have believed that if we could just *understand* what is going on
that we would be okay. We have sought and clutched
on to interpretations and reasons, feeling if we just *knew*
what was really going on or why someone behaved as
they do we would be all right. Yet, when we found an
explanation or interpretation for ourselves or another,
this interpretation, in the long run, really didn't make
much of a difference in the way we felt.

Indeed, if we look carefully at what we are doing,
we just might see that the "understanding" actually resulted in our leaving ourselves and what we were feeling. This understanding helped us abandon ourselves.
Remember being hurt or angry and then thinking that
the feelings were "unjustified" when we "understood"?
Our feelings just are. They will lead us to where we need
to be.

Nobody ever healed by understanding.

Reassurance

Not to worry—

BRIAN

"Not to worry" is a phrase I hear often from an Australian Aboriginal friend of mine. He has one of the most beautiful senses of humor I have ever seen and is often shyly laughing and going ahead with whatever needs to be done. The ease with which he approaches life results in his being easy to be around and also a person I choose to be around as much as possible.

Whenever we are planning something or trying to work something out, he is often peppering the conversation with "Not to worry"! It is almost as if he is adding a dash of reassurance here, a pinch of reassurance there. I find it most interesting that when I am planning something with Brian, *I am reassured*! I know it, whatever it is, *will* work out.

The very fact that I noticed this behavior on his part causes me to pause and wonder how often we really get reassurances in our life. What a great gift reassurances are! They are like quiet celestial erasers of negativity. They don't take away from our having to cope. They just let us know we can cope.

I could become an utterer of reassurances.

Pausing

*It was one of those days so clear, so silent, so still,
you almost feel the earth itself has stopped in
astonishment at its own beauty.*

KATHERINE MANSFIELD

Worriers often have difficulty remembering a day "so clear, so silent, so still" that even the worrying mind stopped for a rest. Yet, they do happen.

When we do stop, many times we look around and realize that we are the only ones rushing around. We realize that the roses, the trees, even the clouds seem suspended in space, and it is as if the universe has paused for a breather. Life has time to experience itself.

Often, when we stop and let ourselves take in the beauty that is around us, we realize that there is much more than we originally imagined. Our eyes begin to see beauty in the cracks in the sidewalk, the crookedness of the tree limbs, the cragginess of faces, even the color of cars.

We don't have to travel to see beauty. It is everywhere.

How much more alive we are when we can feel those times that the earth "has stopped in astonishment at its own beauty."

Bragging/Honesty

I'm worried that none of these blurbs will do you any good!

BETSY MARTIN

Why is it that worriers don't even let themselves stop to know it when they have done something *good*. Betsy Martin did a wonderful job of gathering quotes for this book and . . . worrying about it . . . double productivity.

It is so acceptable to put ourselves down and deny that we have done a good job—"Oh, it was nothing." "Anyone could have done what I did." "I should have spent more time on it." . . . And so it goes.

How long has it been (if ever) that we stood up, looked someone right in the eye, and said, "Yep! I really did a bang-up job on that one"?

We want to think of ourselves as honest persons. Yet, how often are we honest about what we have done *well* and what we have done right?

So often we confuse truth-speaking with bragging. When we have done something well and we admit it, that's truth-speaking. When we have done something well and we don't admit it, that's lying.

I probably need to be more concerned about dishonesty than bragging.

Humility

One reaches all great events of life a virgin.
MARGUERITE YOURCENAR

Our "virginity" in new situations has taken a bum rap!

We have leaned in the direction of believing that being prepared, knowing it all, and being sophisticated are good ways of being. We seek to be "cool."

Yet, what do we miss with this sophistication? We miss the opportunity for true humility. Humility is the openness that puts us in true perspective with ourselves, other human beings, and God. Humility allows for that air of crisp freshness that opens the door for the surprise, the great, the unusual. If we are "cool," we may miss these gifts altogether.

Humility is the root of the "virginity" that allows us to experience life's greatest moments.

Children

How dare you be alive when you've caused me so much worry.

LYNDA

Sometimes it's difficult for our children to translate worry into caring.

Often, when we have worked ourselves into a complete stew worrying about them, when they finally arrive, we jump on them with all four feet. Strange little creatures that they are, they just do not seem to be able to experience our jumping on them as caring!

We need to remember that no one else can "make" us worry. Worrying is one of our choices for reacting to stressful events. Worrying is something we do. For example, when our children do something about which we feel stressed we can: 1) Worry—often our first choice; 2) Pray; 3) Pray and turn it over; 4) Call a friend for support; 5) Admit that we cannot control the situation and that we don't have all the information anyway; 6) Try to stay in the present and deal with whatever comes as it comes; 7) Not give in to crisis and catastrophizing; 8) Focus on what we need to do; 9) Get on with our lives and wait for more information; 10) Go to bed and pull the covers over our head; 11) Sing an aria from our favorite opera.

The choices we have are limitless.

Our children do things and we sometimes fear for them. What we do with that fear is up to us.

Humor

Humor is emotional chaos remembered in tranquillity.

JAMES THURBER

Often, when we are experiencing emotional chaos, we are totally incapable of seeing how funny we are and how funny the situation is. One of the skills that we have developed as human beings is to make the light and simple heavy and serious. We have tried to convince ourselves that nothing that is really important can be funny. We have come to believe that in order to learn something or deal with our lives the situation has to be painful or, at least, *serious.*

Rarely in our moments of emotional chaos do we stop and see how funny we are. And, woe be it if one of our family or friends suggests that our drama might have a lighter side. How dare they make light of possible tragedy!

We need to remember that life is a series of events. We are the ones who turn them into tragedies.

When I can see how funny I am, I have the possibility of seeing how dear I am.

Prayer

If you worry, why pray? If you pray, why worry?
JUNE

It takes practice to get good at prayer, just like anything else, I suppose. When I was in seminary, I learned the proper (head) forms of prayer—invocation, thanksgiving, intercession, praise, and so forth. There seemed to be a belief that all the proper elements needed to be included and that they should come in the proper order. That approach to prayer resulted in such a panic that I never could remember the elements (or feared I couldn't) or their order.

Then I moved to a new level of prayer, carefully asking only for what I needed—not leaving anything out, and including everything that was necessary. So, since I am a nervous flyer—I really like to have my feet on the ground—I started asking for a safe takeoff, a safe flight, and a safe landing (brevity is good—God, after all, is quite busy). This has worked for years, and then I suddenly realized I had left something out—please also, no mechanical problems, no turbulence (just a little would be all right—don't want to ask for too much, do we?) and nothing unusual or dangerous—just a safe, easy flight. Seems to be working. Then I moved to even greater simplicity—Thy will be done (and I'll do my best to get it).

Prayer is simple. We make it difficult.

Wasting Our Time

*Did you ever try to get the waves in the ocean to
do what you want them to? Worry is like that.*

JUNE

As we look back over our lives, we begin to see that the
majority of moments we can truly see as "wasted" are often those in which we have been trying to control
something over which we had absolutely no control.

Surprisingly, as we look back, those moments, days,
weeks when we were actually coping with a horrendous
situation never really seem wasted, although we would
much rather have been doing something else, perhaps.

Even those times when we had nothing to do and we
just let life wash over us never seem wasted in retrospect.

The times that have a tinge of "wastefulness" are
those in which we were more enamored with our illusion of control than we were with our faith in reality.

We are the only ones who can waste our time.

Being Understood

A nod is as good as a wink to a blind horse.

IRISH PROVERB

Have we ever stopped and let ourselves realize how much time we have spent nodding and winking at blind horses?

So often, we believe that it is absolutely essential that others hear what we are saying and understand it completely. If they don't seem to be understanding us, we believe if we just speak more slowly, explain whatever we want them to understand more carefully, and raise the decibels ever so slightly that they will finally get it.

It is important to remember that by our first utterance, we can usually get a pretty good idea if someone has any interest whatsoever in understanding what we are saying. If they have no interest, give up.

If they really want to understand, and just don't get it, try three times . . . and give up.

Nodding, winking, and blabbing when someone has their eyes and ears closed is silly.

Making Love

When I worry about whether our making love will be all right, it isn't.

ANNIE

Lovemaking is one of the gifts of being human. There are many ways to make love. We can make love with someone as we clean up together in the kitchen after a meal.

We can make love as we freely and lovingly let each other go to do what we need to do.

We can make love as we plan a day and a life together. And, we can make love with our bodies coming together out of our deep love for each other.

No matter how we make love, the key element is being present. When we try to plan and control our lovemaking ahead of time in order to make it right, it won't be!

When we worry about our lovemaking being all right when we are doing it, it won't be. We have already left it.

One can never make love if one is not present.

Discontent

*She was poisoned by the fever of her discontent;
brooded over her grievances and misery until they
burst from her, with the violence of physical
nausea.*

KATHARINE SUSANNAH PRICHARD

Discontent is devious. It starts out as a slight uneasiness
in the gut, which we often studiously try to ignore.
Then it builds and moves up through the body and
freezes the heart in its passage. Slowly, ever so slowly, it
slithers its way into our brain, resting quietly when it
first arrives there, lest we discover it and catapult it out
before it takes up residence.

Stealthily it twists and turns until it has set up
housekeeping in our brain and has started reproducing
its own kind to build a living neighborhood of discontent, growing victimization in every garden.

**Remember, our discontent is ours. We can head it
off at the pass.**

Waiting With

We have a lot of anxieties, and one cancels out another very often.

WINSTON CHURCHILL

Learning to wait is one of life's lessons that often seems wasted on the young. Time is often one of the best healers and sorter-outers of our issues. Often, when we do not have a quick solution to a problem, we buck and kick and throw ourselves against the corral of our minds and beings, believing that if we just fling our minds around frantically enough we will find a solution.

We forget that problems and solutions often are not encountered simultaneously. We forget that we are often so distraught when the problem appears that we could not even see that the solution presented itself immediately.

Sometimes, we need to sit with a problem and let it seep into us, without focusing upon it, while we go about our daily work, and we will discover that problems often do, indeed, cancel out one another.

It's hard to hear that "still small voice" when I'm kicking and screaming inside.

Singing Hearts

Ask not what the world needs, ask rather what
makes your heart sing, and go do that, for what
the world needs is people with hearts that sing.

PHILIP THATCHER

We have become so confused, it seems, about living and the real meaning of our lives.

What if the meaning of life is just the living of it? What if the most any of us has to do is to open up to a conscious contact with whatever we call God and live out what is right for us while we prayerfully ask for guidance and support?

We spend so much time trying to figure out what others think we *should* do, and resenting it—what we think others *want* us to do, and resenting it—or what *we* think we *should* do, and resenting it. We have little time in all this confusion to see what it is that truly "makes our hearts sing."

A singing heart could be a great contribution to the universe.

Solutions

Worry gives a small thing a big shadow.
SWEDISH PROVERB

Small things rarely look small when we first encounter them. In fact, for worriers, any unexpected event looms terribly large when first encountered and then gets even larger the longer we dwell on it.

Ah, there's the clue! Can we possibly not dwell on it?

I know a woman who, over the years, has come to serenity by learning not to dwell on things. When something seemingly awful takes her by surprise she goes into her natural state of shock and allows herself to "finger it with her mind" for a while. Then she lets it "sit," unnoticed, and doesn't focus on it for some time, until it has lost its "charge." When it has lost its "charge" for her, the solution has usually emerged, and it is rarely what she would have done under the first impact of the information.

The best solutions are "discovered," not produced.

Being Naughty

Impropriety is the soul of wit.
WILLIAM SOMERSET MAUGHAM

When was the last time you did something naughty—not bad—just naughty? Being good has its rewards and most worriers have long since forgotten the skill of being naughty. We are often too hard on ourselves and those around us. We get to a point where we are terribly serious about almost everything—especially ourselves and our concerns.

Yet, thank goodness, most of us have not completely killed that little spark of naughtiness that hides deep inside of us, just waiting to be fanned. That spark of naughtiness is just waiting for us to let our hair down and be improper for just a minute.

We could walk on the grass—only once, of course. We could really let our laugh go when someone says something hilarious in a fancy restaurant. We could just stop and sit down on a curb for a while when we are tired. We could say what we really think. The possibilities are endless.

Wit is never mean. And, it is often naughty.

Getting High

For me, worrying is like having a drink or eating sugar.

SHEILA

I wonder if we have ever stopped and thought of how much energy we put into getting high each day. Getting high is one of those processes that is rather like the land in the swamp. It looks and even feels good on the surface and, yet, when we step onto it, we find ourselves over our heads in muck.

When we are stressed and concerned about life in general, we often feel dead inside. We begin to wonder if we are really alive and we have doubts that we ever will be again. We need a hit! We need a high! (Or so we believe.)

A high gives us a rush of adrenaline. We feel a surge of energy. We are aware of our bodies and we feel an excitement that, perhaps, we have come to associate with being alive. We get high!

Unfortunately, there is always a drop after getting high, just like the drop we often experience from eating sugar. Worry can affect us just like sugar and alcohol. And, the high doesn't last. The high drains us.

Getting "high" invites "lows."

Entertaining God

My worry lines are God's laughter lines.

ALLISON

It's difficult to think of ourselves as entertainment for God. Yet, if that is our purpose here, we are, indeed, really quite good at it.

Often, it is the people we know—*and love*—who best offer us the most dear, most gentle entertainment. There is something warm and glowing about seeing someone we know thoroughly and love immensely repeat the same foolish behavior over and over again.

When we lay aside our judgment—which is usually easier when we know someone well and love them well—we can have the patience and the distance to see what they do, love them through it, and wait until they discover what they need to discover. In the meantime, we may have a good chuckle or two along the way.

When we think of our mistakes and our foibles as amusing, we may have a glimpse of God.

There could be a worse meaning to my life than entertaining God!

Being "Speedy"

Why is life speeded up so? Why are things so terribly, unbearably precious that you can't enjoy them but can only wait breathless in dread of their going?

ANNE MORROW LINDBERGH

There are so many times when we just wish we could slow down. Remember that wonderful Anthony Newley musical *Stop the World—I Want to Get Off*? I really liked the musical . . . I *loved* the title.

So often it seems that life is in fast forward and all we can do is try to keep up. We rush through those "unbearably precious" moments as if we were picking up dirty clothes, and then wonder why life seems so dull and uninteresting at times. Unfortunately, it seems that everyone around us encourages and expects us to keep going at high speed.

Well, I guess it is up to us, then! Since no one else is going to give us permission to slow down, we are the only ones left.

Life isn't speeded up. We are speeded up.

Hard Lessons

*If . . . you can't be a good example, then you'll
just have to be a horrible warning.*

CATHERINE AIRD

It's important to remember that no matter what we do,
there is always the possibility that we can be an important teacher for someone.

In Kurt Vonnegut's great psychological treatise,
Cat's Cradle, he says that we all go through life as part of
a "karass," or soul group. In that soul group, there are
many people who play various teaching roles for us. The
soul group usually gathers around one or more central
teachers, whom he calls "wampeters." And, some of the
most important teachers we encounter in our passage
through life are "wrang-wrangs." Wrang-wrangs are persons who have very important lessons to teach us and
they teach us these lessons through pain, struggle, and
frustration. We all need wrang-wrangs and we probably
could not learn these lessons in any other way.

*Who knows? I may be a wrang-wrang for someone
and, at least, I'm an important teacher.*

Hallucinating Unreality

I see what a hallucinogen worrying is. Reality this week is nothing like what I was freaked out about last week. The problems I was worried about don't exist. There are some problems that I hadn't thought of. Either way, it's clear to me now that I was living in a false reality when I was worrying.

PETE

How much of our lives are made up of false realities? We start with an idea of what might be and we expand upon that idea. Then, we expand upon the expansion and follow up with additional remodeling and revisions. After a while, the structure we have constructed has little or nothing to do with the reality in which we are living.

When we stick with reality as we are experiencing it right now, we usually can handle it. It's those castles of unreality that are usually difficult to heat and live in during those cold days of distortion.

The unrealities we construct in our minds really do become hallucinations. When we hallucinate, we lose touch with reality.

Reality is often much less scary than our hallucinations.

Having Perspective

*When I get all concerned about something, I stop
and ask myself, "What difference will this make
for the evolution of humankind in the next ten
thousand years?" and I get my perspective back.*

ANNE WILSON SCHAEF

The ability to have a perspective on a situation is one of
the most fragile gifts we have in this life. In fact, our
perspective is destroyed completely by fear, drama, excitement, anxiety, intensity, and, of course, most of all
by adrenaline.

We all want to be useful to ourselves and others.
We want to have wise counsel to share at just the right
time. (Of course, *wanting* to be wise is one of those
other elements that can so easily destroy the thread of
perspective!) We want to be able to recognize the muck
before we plunge headlong into it.

Yet, none of these wonderful attributes is possible unless we give ourselves time to step back and re-weave our
gossamer thread of perspective so we can hang on to it.

**Our perspective is fragile and, luckily, it is easily re-
built.**

Simplicity

ABORIGINAL HEALING PRAYER

Spit him out all that rubbish worry.
Come on in
All way in
You Good Spirit Air.

ABORIGINAL WOMAN ELDER

One beautiful characteristic of so many Aboriginal people is that they get right to the point. They don't spend a lot of time getting bogged down in analyzing, interpreting, or trying to "understand." When they *do* speak, they just say it like it is. How refreshing to go right to the point.

We really don't have to spend a lot of time fooling around with worry. We don't need to study it, read what the experts say, or have a thorough analysis (even if we would *like* to have all this information). We can just spit worry out and focus upon filling our minds and bodies with "Good Spirit Air."

In Zen Buddhism when one focuses on the simple act of breathing, all else falls into place.

Self-Esteem

*All you are left with during a crisis is your
conduct during it.*

JOHNNIE COCHRAN

Two of the most important treasures we have in life are
our relationship with our Creator, or God, and our relationship with ourselves. Both are facts of our existence
and both can be ignored or tampered with for long periods of time.

Crisis times are opportunities that life gives us to
see where we really stand. A time of crisis offers us the
opportunity to slip into behaviors we do not like in ourselves or others, and feel justified in doing so. Whenever we can adopt the victim role for ourselves, we feel
justified in becoming perpetrators. If someone is trying
to "get us," we use the occasion to feel perfectly justified
in "getting them."

What a lapse of our self-esteem! After all the dust
clears, all we really have left is ourselves. We have to
live with ourselves. Hopefully, we have acted in such a
way as to maintain a good relationship with our Creator
and ourselves.

**When I like and trust myself, everything else seems to
fall into place.**

Our Bodies

Never eat more than you can lift.

MISS PIGGY

So many of our worries center around our weight and our bodies. We are either too fat (usually) or too skinny, too tall or too short, too full or too flat. We are never quite right.

Obsessing about our bodies has become a national pastime and is encouraged and supported by a great industry.

Have we ever just stopped to notice how wonderful our bodies are, whatever they look like? Our bodies house us and carry us around. Our bodies have feelings that give us information and keep us alive. Our bodies store memories, good and bad, which are available when we are ready for them. Our bodies give us sexual and sensual pleasures, and one of these pleasures is eating.

When we listen to our bodies, they tell us what we need and what is good for us. We may, however, need hearing aids for body communications.

Worry is like wax in my inner ears.

Responding

*Even when I do pray, my first reaction is to
worry.*

CONNIE

One of the important lessons that life teaches is to wait
through our first reaction. Very few of us are capable of
always having a clear response to surprises. How long it
takes us to learn that our instant body reaction may
only be a primitive survival reaction, and we may not be
dealing with a survival issue at all.

If we get through our first knee-jerk, then our next
unreliable response may be to *think* about the issue. Unfortunately, our thinking has been known to be just as
useless as our instant visceral response.

If we have survived the first two onslaughts, we
then have a good possibility of our next response, which
can usually be more functional and helpful than the first
two. . . . We can wait with our knowing and take the
time to *discover* the response that is truest to ourselves
and best for us.

**We must remember—we have time to be good to our-
selves and others.**

Being Happy

If you really want to be happy, nobody can stop you.
SISTER MARY TRICKY

So often, we are afraid to risk being happy. Strange, isn't it, that being happy can be seen as a risk? There are all sorts of dangers involved.

We have discovered that there are people around us who are suspicious of happy people . . . they just can't be trusted. Then, there are others who seem openly to resent happiness and seem determined to squash it at every turn. After all, if one person is happy, doesn't this reflect upon those who aren't and, invisibly, put some kind of pressure on everyone else to be happy, too? At the very least, a happy person demonstrates that happiness is possible and, if it's possible, then isn't it available to everyone?

Then, there are our own qualms . . . it will go away . . . it won't last . . . it will make us vulnerable. By the time we get through all these issues, happiness has gone.

We do, however, as human beings have the potential and the right to be happy. Indeed, there's a rumor going around that happiness is what the Creator had in mind for us.

My happiness is up to me. I don't have to make it happen. The potential is always there within me.

Underestimating Ourselves

*Worry is like spinning your wheels in the snow—
the rut gets deeper but there's no forward motion.*

SUE WHITAKER

Let's face it, sometimes we just don't *want* any forward motion. We have come to feel safer with paralysis, and any kind of forward motion would scare us to death. After all, when a forward motion lurches us out of paralysis, we can never tell in what direction we will go.

Worry can help us try to keep our lives like comfortable old shoes. Old shoes have their drawbacks and at least we know what those drawbacks are.

Of course, we get scared sometimes. The new always carries with it the fear of the unfamiliar. Sooo—it's okay to be scared. Feel the fear. Go into it. Explore it. Usually we can come out the other side. As long as we try to keep ourselves immobilized, we will never find out what we can do.

When we underestimate ourselves, we are insulting God.

Awe

I share Einstein's affirmation that anyone who is not lost in the rapturous awe at the power and glory of the mind behind the universe "is as good as a burnt out candle."

MADELEINE L'ENGLE

Often, our lives become so crowded and clamoring that we become too busy and burnt out for awe and wonder. Our minds have become so busy that we have no room for the beautiful, the unexpected.

A friend of mine shared with me a recent encounter that he had with a snake as he was taking a walk through the woods. He had never seen a snake in the wild before and he was filled with awe as it slithered across the path on which he was walking. He described the beautiful iridescent colors of the snake's body and its effortless dance of movement as it made its way into the woods. Others asked if he was afraid and his answer was, "I was so filled with awe: I had no time for fear."

May our lives be so filled with awe that we have no time for fear.

Insulting God

*If our faith delivers us from worry, then our worry
is an insult flung in the face of God.*

ROBERT RUNCIE,
ARCHBISHOP OF CANTERBURY

Only recently have I begun to recognize how I regularly and even daily insult God. Whenever I think I am not good enough, wish I were different, or believe I am not up to the job God seems to have given me, I am insulting God.

When I do not accept others the way they are and judge their peculiarities, their idiosyncrasies, their "strange" beliefs, or their "wrong" way of doing things, I am insulting God and the unfathomable artistry behind creation.

When I do not trust that my life and the lives of those I love are steadfastly and surely in the gentle hands of the Creator, I am insulting God.

I have only to do my legwork. I need to keep as clear and in touch with myself and my Creator as I can, and leave the rest up to God.

Of course, many times all this trusting the process of the universe is easier said than done. Yet, I truly don't want to insult God.

When I see the ways I insult God, I have a chance to grow and change.

Our History

A people without history is like the wind on the buffalo grass.

LAKOTA SAYING

Today might be a good time for us to set aside our day-to-day cares and worries and to let ourselves notice that we did not spring full-blown from the head of Zeus. We in the modern culture have often been critical of Native peoples for recognizing their ancestors, and have cynically called their remembering "ancestor worship."

However, let's stop for just a moment and let ourselves recognize that without our ancestors *we wouldn't be here.* It's as simple as that—biologically, we would not be here. We may not have liked our parents or even our grandparents *and* without them, quite simply, we would not be here.

The biology is easy to accept, and there are those other, almost imperceptible transmissions from our heritage that filter down to us in unknown ways that affect who we are and what we do.

None of us is truly "self-made." We have a history. We have a heritage. Pondering the meaning of our history informs our living.

Escape from Intimacy

Worry is a great use of my time. It keeps me from intimacy with those I love. It keeps me from getting "too much" sleep. It's even an excellent way to "while away the hours." Worry is like an old friend.

BETH

What does it mean to escape from intimacy? Why are we so ready to escape from intimacy?

So often, we have devised ingenious ways of escaping from ourselves. We have used "niceness" to avoid letting ourselves know what is truly important for us. We have shut off our feelings and our knowings. We find ourselves afraid to admit that "we don't want to talk right now" or "we don't want you to ride with us" because we need some alone time. We escape from intimacy with ourselves and, consequently, have no intimacy with others.

Worry can be like a drug that pulls us away from ourselves and others. We can use worry, work, and many other of our favorite "ploys" for progressive isolation and withdrawal.

Escaping from intimacy is setting up life in such a way as to miss it.

Today might be a very good day to stop and explore what we use to escape from intimacy.

Managing Life

Life is so constructed as to be "unmanageable."
ANNE WILSON SCHAEF

Most of us have a great terror of our lives becoming unmanageable. We fancy ourselves immobilized in some hospital bed with tubes coming out of every orifice. An unmanageable life is just too terrifying for words and is indicative of hopelessness and decay.

But, what if life is actually constructed to be unmanageable? What if life is set up in such a way that we really can't control it or much of anything, and our most important learning is not in how to manage life but in knowing that we can't?

Believing that we can manage our lives may be one of the greatest of human follies, and our parents and teachers have been teaching us the wrong lessons. Life itself may be so constructed as to be unmanageable and we have the opportunity to participate in it. It's as simple as that.

In trying to develop the skills to manage my life, I may have been missing my life.

Prayer

"Worry" is used much more frequently than
"pray," at least in the business world; yet they
both are ways of hoping a troubling situation will
be happily resolved.

BETSY MARTIN

In the business world and in the business of our lives, we are always looking for ways to get a happy resolution to issues that are troubling us. We try to arm ourselves with skills that will suffice in time of need. We plan, we figure out, we try to understand, we look at different angles, we anticipate, we control, we manipulate, we compromise, we stretch the truth, and then, often, we worry.

Did you ever think about praying? I know some of us have a huge load of excess baggage that we have collected over the years about prayer. We hear the word and we envision some sanctimonious old fart in whom we have never had any trust anyway intoning words to a God with whom we have long since lost touch, and our faces turn into a twisted pout: "Right!"

Yet, prayer can be a very simple and very truthful "I don't know what to do now. Help!" End of message.

Sometimes, the old things can work if we face them with new attitudes.

Family History

*I don't feel I choose worry. It is part of my history
that comes together in worry.*

BETTY

Worry is intergenerational. Worry is a process and an
attitude that is passed down from parents to child and is
often as deeply ingrained as our genes.

However, the good news about worry is that, unlike
our genes, if it is learned, it can be unlearned. We don't
have to carry everything that we have learned from our
parents with us for a lifetime. We can unlearn what we
want to drop.

The first step is to see that worry has become a
problem for us. Never underestimate how enormous this
step is!

Then, after we have recognized that worry is a
problem, we need to see if we are truly *willing* to let it
go. If we are not truly willing to let worry go, we may as
well stop right there and hang in with worrying for a
few more years.

If we are truly willing to let it go, we can turn it
over. Turning it over doesn't mean that we *will* it to go.
Willing usually doesn't work.

Turning it over means that we simply let it go, with
no guarantee that we can take it back whenever we want.

**I don't have to repeat my family's history and I have to
be willing to let it go.**

Learning

—Not to create a crisis;
—Not to prevent a crisis if it is in the natural
course of events.

ANONYMOUS, AL-ANON

These two learnings from Al-Anon are an absolute balm for worriers.

Have we ever stepped back to see how much of our worrying goes into creating a crisis? On the surface, we may believe that our worrying is an attempt to prevent a crisis; yet, have we been open to seeing how the worry itself is an occasion for stirring things up?

If we aren't unconsciously creating a crisis, is our worrying really a meddling in someone else's life, trying somehow to prevent a "natural course of events" that they have set up for themselves?

Do we have a somewhat misguided idea that love is trying to save someone from themselves? Are we interfering with their learning what they need to learn from the decisions they have made and getting on with their lives?

My old way of loving may need some revamping.

Traveling

To travel hopefully is a better thing than to arrive,
and the true success is to labour.
ROBERT LOUIS STEVENSON

Travel offers so many opportunities for a worrier, especially if we believe that the purpose of travel is to get there.

I had a friend who was diagnosed with cancer. She surrounded herself with a huge flurry of experts and information-givers. In a rare moment of quiet, I asked her what she would do if she knew that she only had a month or so to live. She mentioned several members of her family and friends with whom she would like to spend time and said that she would like to go for long walks on the beach. Then . . . she went on to say that she just wanted to get these six months of chemotherapy over so she could do these things and get on with her life.

I think she missed the point.

The issue is not in the length of the journey. The issue is in how we travel it.

Paradox

We have to believe in free will. We've got no choice.

ISAAC BASHEVIS SINGER

Isaac Bashevis Singer is one of my favorite writers. He writes of mists and myths, spooks and spirits, history and fantasy, all coming out of a rich Jewish heritage and tradition. His stories are often gripping and bone-chilling and, most of all, while they often appear to be simple folktales, they are usually complex.

So, why *wouldn't* he say we have no choice but to believe in free will? Of course, in simple words, he again throws us the complexity of paradox. If we have no choice, how can we have free will, and if we have free will, how can we not have a choice? And . . . such is life.

Often the key to life is living the paradox. Our modern world has tried to reduce our choices to simple "this or that" dualisms and has missed the meaning of life.

Living the paradox is more than this or that.

Sex

I don't want to control anybody's mind or anybody's heart—I just want to help free people from the concept of sex as evil instead of a gift from God.

MARY CALDERONE

Sex is one of those areas where confusion reigns and fear triumphs. Unfortunately, we live in a society that is very unclear about, and very obsessed with, sex. We have societal support to choose sex as one of the most important focus areas for worry. We have become overwhelmed with the "shoulds," ours and others', and we have little or no idea what is right for us.

Let's forgive ourselves a little bit on this topic. We have had a lot of help in becoming as confused as we are. We didn't get here alone.

A well-known Hawaiian kahuna has been heard to say, "You should have sex every day with a righteous partner." One couple who have a beautiful relationship and a very happy sex life say, "Sex is like brushing our teeth. It is a happy part of living."

There are three important things to remember about sex. We should only be sexual when 1) we are clear about it; 2) the other person is clear about it; 3) the situation is clear. Otherwise, celibacy is a viable option for a while.

Amusement

The main obligation is to amuse yourself.
S. J. PERELMAN

How often do we say—and mean it—"I'm happy!"? Are we even aware what truly amuses us in this life? A few years ago, I decided to spend time only with people who delight in my company. Making this decision doesn't mean that I don't interact with others or that I am not cordial to others. What it does mean is that I realize that my time is very precious and valuable to me and when I do have time to spend with others, I spend it with those who delight in me and in whom I delight. While this does mean that I have quit spending time with some people, I still find the number of people included in this category more than enough.

So often we have forgotten how to amuse ourselves and with whom to amuse ourselves. We expect to be thrilled or entertained and we have forgotten about amusement. Amusement is quieter than thrill or entertainment. Amusement is active. We rarely can just sit back and passively watch and be truly amused. We have to participate more actively to be amused.

Remember, as a child, watching the antics of an ant trying to get home with a treasure? We were amused.

Choices

I discovered I always have choices and sometimes it's only a choice of attitude.

JUDITH M. KNOWLTAN

One of the most terrifying and paralyzing situations a human being can face is not having choices or, at least, believing we don't have choices. Believing we don't have choices is like entering a self-constructed prison with no windows or doors and then wondering how we got there. The walls of believing we don't have choices easily transform themselves into slides, plunging us into victimdom.

Unfortunately, the walls of victimdom are much more slippery than those of not having choices. When we become victims we can slide further into our tunnel-like prison structure. We become angry and willing to lash out and make anyone suffer for what has "happened" to us, refusing to see that we had choices and made choices early on.

Knowing that I have choices and that my attitude about my experiences can save me from slippery prisons can change the way I experience my life.

Mana

*I can't sleep at night, because even at night I'm
worrying about things and planning things. It's the
mana, you see. If you've got it, it never leaves
you alone. You have to be thinking about the
people and working for them, all the time.*

DAME WHINA COOPER

Dame Whina Cooper was a feisty old lady who recently
died at the age of ninety-seven. She had loved and
served her people well. A Maori in New Zealand, she
was keenly aware of the rights and needs of her people
and she "gave her all" until her death. If there was one
fact in the universe about which Dame Whina had no
question, it was her personal mana, or power. She knew
she had personal power and she knew where to put it.

Each of us has mana. Whether we recognize it or
not, we are gifted with personal power, and part of our
task in life is to recognize our mana and know how to
use it in a way that is beneficial to ourselves and others.

It is an insult to the Creator to ignore or refuse to
admit our mana. We can give ourselves all kinds of excuses, like: "I'm just like everyone else." "I don't want to
be conceited." "I'm not good enough."—and so on and
so on. And, the truth of it is, we are unique, and as we
become who we are our mana appears and grows.

*I have personal power. To refuse to admit it is ridicu-
lous. To use it to lord over others is unforgivable.*

Taking Stock

A trout in the pot is better than a salmon in the sea.
IRISH PROVERB

Worriers have a terrible time stopping and honestly taking stock of our lives. We find it so easy to dwell on the negative and what *might* happen that, sometimes, taking a good, hard, honest look at what *is* seems completely inconceivable.

When we are in this negative frame of mind, taking stock usually has a bit of a "downer" tinge to it. Sometimes it helps to be reminded that taking stock is just that—looking at the whole picture, not only half of it.

Today might be a good day to take stock. Okay, so we're worriers and we want to start out with what's wrong. Go ahead! Put it down! List all those fears: what might happen, and what we can't control, and what we can't solve right now. Sometimes it helps to see things in writing.

Then . . . now, I know this might be difficult . . . and . . . give it a try . . . put down the things in our lives that are going just fine. We may think of simple things like: our bowels work well . . . we like our friends . . . a new day welcomed us this morning . . . we heard the wind. (Perhaps we needed some help on the *good* ones!)

When we take stock, we must watch out for our negative biases.

Self-Abuse

I tend also to approach a problem by looking at the worst-case scenario and when I know what it is, then I can work out a manner of dealing with it. I'm not good with surprises or letting things go and then doing last-minute kinds of things. In that sense, it's beneficial to me because if I worry about something happening, I'll have it figured out (e.g., where the baby can get special education or something like that).

NANCY

Self-abuse comes in many forms. Rarely do we see how self-abusive it is to force ourselves to look at the worst possible thing that could happen, when we have little or no information that we are dealing with reality. Focusing upon the worst possibility is a clear case of self-torture hiding under the guise of preparedness.

Perhaps we have become so inured to our self-abuse that we do not even recognize that we are doing it. We give self-abuse other labels, such as concern, caring, preparation, and planning, and we batter ourselves mercilessly.

Unfortunately, when we become accustomed to abusing ourselves we can quite easily move into abusing others and not even realize we are doing it.

Self-abuse never stops with just myself.

Truth

The best mind-altering drug is truth.

LILY TOMLIN

Rarely do we let ourselves stop and realize the far-reaching implications that truth has upon us. Something happens inside of us when we speak the truth. A shift takes place in our minds, and our bodies, somehow, seem to shift into being taller and straighter.

Speaking the truth lets us know who we are and opens the way for others to *see* us intimately. When we speak the truth, our energy starts to rebuild as we know that we will not have to put energy into maintaining the lie.

Truth is like a celestial enema that refreshes our souls and in so doing alters our minds and the way we see our world.

We have many opportunities every day to test out truth-speaking. It's up to us.

Trouble

Don't meet troubles halfway.

PROVERB

It's not like we don't have enough to do!

For most of us life offers a full plate. In fact, most of us find that we have constructed our lives in such a way that we have more than enough to do. We like to keep busy ... and in keeping busy ... believe that we are worthwhile. Does our worth really reside in our busyness?

We have so many things we can do with our time, why on earth would we go out looking for trouble? Why not let trouble come to us, if it needs to do that? Perhaps, just perhaps, if we do not go out to meet it, it will hit a detour sign before it gets to us, or maybe it will decide the road to us is too rocky or filled with potholes and not worth the effort or ... maybe this particular trouble just wasn't meant for us, anyway.

In the meantime, we can take a long bath, pumice our feet, go for a walk, fiddle with the car, or sit and stare. The options are endless.

Why go looking for trouble when there are so many other activities with which to occupy our time?

Perspectives

There is nothing either good or bad but thinking makes it so.

WILLIAM SHAKESPEARE

Why is it that the same situation—let's take something as painful as the death of a child—can be experienced in such opposite ways by two different people or families? For one family, the death of a child is a horror and a personal disaster beyond words. The death of a child is the end of the world and something that truly substantiates our victim role for life.

For another family, the death of a child is sad and they grieve the loss *and* they focus on the gift of the child in their lives and the learnings and tremendous pleasures and opportunities that child has opened for them. They see life in terms of gifts and learnings, and death as a part of life. Death is a gift itself.

Neither of these families is *wrong*. Each does what it does with an event. Yet, they teach us the power of accepting life on life's terms.

My life is what I make it.

Worrying to God

I realized when I was praying for water for Dolly that I was actually "worrying to God"—I noticed myself praying like this before—when a friend was in labor a prolonged time—I "worried" her to God.

CONNIE

How often do we "worry to God"? And, what does this mean to us?

Real prayer, it seems, is based upon faith, and the bottom line of faith is trusting that things will always work out as they should.

When we worry to God, we don't trust that God may have a little more information about the situation than we do. We "worry to God" and that "worrying" is really based upon our belief that we know better than God how everything *should* come out and we would like God to be our *assistant* in making this happen.

In fact, we usually can run the world, especially our world, quite effectively by ourselves, and we see God as a kind of celestial doorman who opens the door and helps us with our bags only if we need it. The rest of the time, we can manage quite nicely on our own, thank you! (We would like to be assured that our "doorman" is on twenty-four-hour call and strong and alert at all times, just in case.)

Pay attention, God—we might need you sometime.

Remembrance

*You can guess, nevertheless, that we had a fairly
good time there when we were young, when we
were young enough not to worry about our place
in the world or what was happening outside us.*
JOHN ALAN EDWARD MULGAN

Remember being "young enough not to worry about our
place in the world or what was happening outside us"?
One of the truly beautiful gifts of being human is that
we can remember. Our bodies store memories that even
our brains don't know we have.

A dubious gift—you might say. Yet, even the remembering of the traumatic and so-called bad things
gives us the opportunity to work them through at the
times in our lives when we have more strength, more
perspective, more wisdom, and more experience. What
a gift this storing of old memories is when we realize
that we have within us the ability to work through
whatever has happened to us.

Then, there is the remembrance of the "good" experiences. If we can remember "not worrying about our
place in the world or what was happening outside us,"
we have an easy possibility of returning to that way of
functioning.

**The miracle of remembrance is a gift of being human.
I have the option of using it wisely.**

Rules and Laws

To be properly wicked, you do not have to break
the law, just follow it to the letter.
ANTHONY DE MELLO

Worriers are always concerned about the rules and the
laws. We don't always like or agree with the rules and we
certainly do not want to get in trouble. Sometimes, this
way of operating puts us in a bind, and we let ourselves
slip into a mode of getting away with whatever we can
while still staying within the rules or the law. Unfortunately, this mode of operating doesn't relieve our worry.
We know that we aren't breaking the law and there is a
modicum of relief in that. And, at the same time, we discover that following the law to the letter often leads us
into areas where we don't quite feel easy with ourselves.
On a deeper level, we are restless. We keep feeling that
we are getting away with something and we keep looking over our shoulder waiting to be caught while our
rational brain says, "It's legal. Relax!"

We need to stop and see what's important to us.
We may "get away with something" and is the wear and
tear on our insides worth it? I doubt it.

When I feel I am getting away with something, I don't
feel good or easy with myself. Nothing is worth making
me feel bad about myself.

Being a Burden

*Knowing that one is the target of another's worries
often lays a heavy burden on that targeted one.*

BETSY MARTIN

Why is it that when we try the hardest to be loving and caring, our behavior often seems to backfire?

We love our kids and our families and friends and we truly only want the best for them. We may slip into thinking that we know what the best for them is occasionally *and* we truly do care about them and want them to be healthy and happy. We are all clear about that. We may not, however, be clear about the best way to go about our caring.

We have been taught that worry is a form of loving and if we don't worry about those who are dear to us, we don't really care about them. Maybe we need to stop and take a long, hard look at what we have been taught.

When we look at some of the messages and teachings we have gleaned from dysfunctional families and a dysfunctional society, lo and behold, we find that many of the teachings themselves are DYSFUNCTIONAL! Surprise! Surprise!

We don't want to be a burden to those we love, now . . . do we?

Words

Man does not live by words alone, despite the fact that sometimes he has to eat them.

ADLAI STEVENSON

Words and thoughts ofttimes seem to be our favorite fodder. We convince ourselves that words, thoughts, ideas, and concepts are real. We forget that all these contraptions are just abstractions and are only as real as we allow them to be.

Someone can say, "I hate you," and we can stand back and look at them in startled disbelief, shrug our shoulders, *see* what a fool they are, turn on our heel, and walk away. Another can say, "I hate you," and we can take in those words, roll them around, sit with them for a while, and spit them out on the ground, knowing these words have nothing to do with us. Then, someone else can say, "I hate you," and we can believe them and be truly sorry they feel this way. Still, yet again, a person can say, "I hate you," and we can take those words inside, turn them on ourselves, poison ourselves with them, and decide we are awful persons. It's up to us what we do with the words that come at us.

> *Sticks and stones*
> *Will break my bones*
> *But words*
> *Will never hurt me*
> *(I can hurt me, though)*

Destiny

*The closer one gets to realizing his destiny, the
more that destiny becomes his true reason for
being.*

PAULO COELHO

What an old-fashioned term—our destiny! We have become almost too sophisticated to think in terms of destiny. We are too much in control to think of our lives being guided or that we have a purpose for being here.

Yet, we like to read about destiny. We love novels and stories where the heroine/hero struggles against their destiny or searches to find their destiny. Somehow, we are always relieved when the person surrenders, accepts their destiny, and everything begins to fall into place.

Why have we come to insist that the concept of destiny needs to stay in the realm of a fairy tale?

When we open ourselves to what is truly right for us in our lives and we accept the support and guidance that are available for us at all times all around us, we begin to open ourselves to our destiny. We begin to have a glimpse of our "true reason for being."

What is right for me is right for me. What is right for others is right for them. I only need to be open to what is right for me and live it a step at a time.

Money/Self-Image

A pound of care will not pay an ounce of debt.

PROVERB

Money, debts, mortgages, bills, responsibilities—these are, indeed, a favorite focus for worry. We all want to be responsible and we especially want to be responsible about money matters, and that's not always easy.

One of the ways we prove to ourselves that we are responsible about money matters is to worry about them. Even if we can do nothing about our financial situation, we have convinced ourselves that we can demonstrate our good faith by worrying about our debts.

Nice try. Worry has never generated a dime! In fact, it often keeps us from what we want to do the most, which is to be productive.

Have we ever thought that our worry about our money matters has a lot more to do with maintaining our self-image to ourselves and others than it has to do with paying the bills? Certainly, it won't hurt to take a look at this angle anyway.

When maintaining my self-image interferes with my reality, I need to stop and see what's really important to me.

Moments

The past has flown away. The coming month and year do not exist. Ours only is the present's tiny point.

MOHMUD SHABISTARI

My wealth is in moments! Each moment brings the precious possibility of living as a new creation.

Life is made up of moments. Each moment is freely given to us by the Creator and it is ours to spend as we see fit.

We came into this world with a huge savings account of moments and we have enough to spend some foolishly, waste some, and squander others with there still being more to come.

We also have the possibility of seeing each one as a treasure magnanimously given, which is ours to use for our growth and awareness. We can spend each moment in awareness of the immense gift that it is.

Oddly enough, moments cannot be hoarded or saved for a rainy day. They don't keep well and they wither when we attempt to hold on to them.

Moments are gifts. Moments are life.

Forcing Creativity

*A poem may be worked over once it is in being,
but may not be worried into being.*

ROBERT FROST

Can anything be "worried into being"? I doubt it.

Robert Frost had his finger on a pulse of creativity. We want to be creative and we believe we can produce and control creativity at will.

We cannot make creativity happen any more than we can make a new day happen. We seem to forget, at times, that creativity is a gift of life. We cannot force a new poem into being any more than we can worry a new day into being. Both are gifts!

Basically, we are struggling with a problem of trust. We simply have trouble believing that anything will happen if we don't *make* it happen. We have come to trust force. We have difficulty trusting trust.

The problem with forcing things is that they often become misshapen in the process. This misshaping can happen to ourselves, our children, our poems, or our lives.

Creativity comes from a place beyond ourselves.

Decisions/Being Free/Courage

Decision is a risk rooted in the courage of being free.

PAUL TILLICH

We rarely think of ourselves as courageous persons. We think of courage as something that is the possession of heroes and persons much beyond us in life and living.

One of Paul Tillich's greatest books is *The Courage to Be*. He understood that just "being" took a barrelful of courage at every turn. To be free, truly free, is to make decisions and, in living, we make thousands of decisions every day. We decide (really!) when to get up or to go to bed. We decide what to wear, what to eat, what we'll say, how we'll say it. We may not see ourselves as decisive and we make many, many decisions every day.

In fact, the courage of making our decisions and living with them gives us the freedom to be. It is the freedom to be that gives us the courage of being free.

When we refuse to make decisions or we want others to make them for us and then be victims, we forfeit our "courage to be free."

My decisions may not always be good ones, yet when I own them I am free.

Winning

Yesterday I dared to struggle. Today I dare to win.
BERNADETTE DEVLIN

Struggle is okay. Struggle is acceptable. Everyone admires someone who struggles. Indeed, strugglers are usually not a threat to anyone. Everyone likes a struggler. If our lives are going well, we can even feel a little superior to a struggler and offer them a helping hand now and again.

But winning . . . now that's another matter entirely. Winners are open season. Lots of people would like to pick off a winner just for the fun of it. You know how it is! It's sort of like eating the heart of a warrior. It gives one power to wipe out a winner . . . or, at least, we are afraid others believe it does.

We can worry a lot about winning. Winning takes a lot of courage. Personal winning takes even more courage because it is not based on win-lose. Daring to run the risk of winning as a person is scary business . . . and . . . well worth the risk.

I have the courage to struggle. Do I dare risk succeeding?

Taking the Leap

I'm glad to hear you're doing a book on worrying.
I have learned a lot about my worrying lately.

SHEILA

Writing a book about worry can generate a good deal of worry. Will the topic be broad enough for a whole book? Are people interested in worry? Are people so attached to their worry that they have no interest in letting go of it? Will people get angry with the insinuation that there might maybe possibly perhaps be options to worrying? What would happen if the thirteen million worriers in the U.S. all gave up worrying at once?

You see the problem here. Worrying an issue is one of the most effective methods we have of not dealing with it. When we decide to go ahead and grapple with the issue, the worries can actually provide grist for the creative mill. We can never imagine where our next ideas will come from unless we are willing to take the leap and plunge into new ideas.

Writing a book about worry is much like the spider spinning a new web. The spider spins down a long thread and then launches itself into the breezes, trusting that as it swings on that gossamer thread it will land someplace where it can attach the other end of the web and start building. Writing is somewhat like the leap of the spider. Life is the spider's leap.

When we are willing to leap we may land where we can build something.

Making Light of Difficulties

He manga wai kia kore e whitikia.

It is a big river indeed that cannot be crossed.

MAORI SAYING

It seems redundant to say that everyone is going to have difficulties. The issue is not whether or not we have difficulties in life. The issue is how we handle them. All of us have rivers to cross. We have to deal with getting or not getting promotions. We have to deal with death—of those close to us, and ultimately our own. We have to deal with money—what we do with it and what it does to us. There's no end to the list of what we have to deal with in this life. At least, this is one issue on which we can agree—life *is* dealing with life.

We need to look at how we face difficulties. This old Maori saying suggests to us that we can make light of difficulties and they will disappear, or we can blow them up until they begin to reproduce. The choice is ours.

Difficulties will often evaporate if I don't keep pumping life into them.

Sorrow

*Ah! if you only knew the peace there is in an
accepted sorrow.*

JEANNE DE LA MOTTE-GUYTON

Why is it we fight experiencing our sorrow so? In some
ways, my sorrow reminds me of the depth of my ability
to love.

Some of us are not so sure about our ability to love.
We may not have grown up in very loving families and
simply did not have role models who taught us how to
love. Or, we may have been hurt by others and are fearful of taking the risk of loving. Or, maybe nothing we
ever do is quite good enough for us and the ability to
love is just another item we have chucked into that
category. Whatever the reason, we may have come to
doubt that we can truly love another person. Even
when we fear we have not developed or have lost our
ability to love, we probably have not lost our ability to
feel sorrow.

When we accept our sorrow and let ourselves feel
our sorrow, we gain the peace that comes from knowing
our loving.

**My sorrow may be the passage to experiencing my
ability to love.**

Feeling Our Feelings

Before The Cherry Orchard *was sold everybody was worried and upset, but as soon as it was all settled finally and once for all, everybody calmed down, and felt quite cheerful.*

ANTON CHEKHOV

We often worry about how we will react to a situation when we have absolutely no idea what our real reaction will be when the event actually happens.

Some of us worriers see our worry as preparation and practice, and hope that our worrying will help us deal with the situation better since we have been rehearsing. . . . Maybe!

Yet, let's look at another possibility. What if our worrying has us so rehearsed for the feeling that we are just *sure* we will feel, we have left no real opening for the unanticipated feelings we are *actually* experiencing? What if our worrying has, indeed, robbed us of our ability to cope and even may rob us of some positive feelings we may have that we never could have anticipated? The possibilities are limitless.

My worrying may be getting in the way of me.

Uniqueness

I am not eccentric. It's just that I am more alive
than most people. I am an unpopular electric eel
set in a pond of goldfish.

DAME EDITH SITWELL

Aren't we great! We're not weird! We're not eccentric! We are just unique in a world that has the mistaken idea that conformity is somehow better.

So what if we want to mix antique and modern in our homes? So what if we like both classical and rock music? So what if we have ideas that are "unusual"? These ideas could also be viewed as "cutting edge" if seen by the right person.

Our style of dress may even be seen as having a certain flair. Unfortunately, an electric eel gives off so much energy that goldfish get frightened, but that's not the fault of the eel, now, is it?

We might even find that other people begin to value our uniqueness, if we treasure it ourselves.

I don't have to be anyone but myself, which is quite enough in itself, thank you.

Taking Inventory/Borrowing

*A worried man could borrow a lot of trouble with
practically no collateral.*

HELEN NIELSEN

Borrowing is an interesting process with or without collateral. We borrow when we believe we do not have enough or when we want more than we have.

It's so easy to fall into the frame of mind that we don't have enough or that we aren't enough. Maybe we need to stop and look carefully at what we do have and what we need, instead of focusing on what we do not think we have.

Everyone needs to take stock once in a while. Businesses that don't take inventory cannot function well. Unfortunately, when we are worried, we are usually not good inventory-takers. Our worry pushes us in the direction of believing that we should be able to control people, processes, and events over which we have no control whatsoever, and we end up becoming unrealistic and borrowing more and more trouble to try to control the uncontrollable, and feeling impoverished in the process. Our feelings have become our collateral.

Thank goodness we have options! We can step out of the worry frenzy and see what we really need. We can see what we have power over and what we don't. We cannot afford to go into emotional debt.

**When I don't borrow trouble, I don't have so many
emotional debts.**

Never

Never trouble trouble till trouble troubles you.

PROVERB

Never look for something you do not need to do
Never put your trust in one on whom you can't rely
Never try to be someone which, for you, would be a lie
Never try to control something that cannot be controlled
Never worry about aging, or the process of becoming
  old
Never try to run the lives of children you hold dear
Never try to live a life completely based on fear
Never try to make okay that which simply is not
Never try to cover up something you have just forgot
Never act as if you are doing this life yourself
Remember you have to participate and there's really lots
  of help

Never forget to remember that you can have some fun.
You don't have to make trouble to do it, only let it come.

Peace

A crust eaten in peace is better than a banquet partaken in anxiety.

AESOP

One of the questions we worriers have to ask ourselves is if we can tolerate letting ourselves have some peace. Are we willing to let go of the adrenaline rush and just let some peace settle into our lives for a few minutes?

There are many opportunities for peace in a normal day. Waking up in the morning can be a peaceful, quiet time. We can let ourselves identify with the sunrise.

Sunrise doesn't happen all at once, you know, regardless of what the papers say. Sunrise is a slow, gradual process of easing into the day. As the night graciously, slowly begins to pull back its protective cloak of shadow, the faint coral lining begins to peek out, backlit by a million stars ready to bow to the warmth of the returning sun. Night caringly moves in to offer rest to another part of the planet while the songs of birds pull in the color of morning.

The peacefulness of the process of morning is ours for the embracing.

I am surrounded by peace if I choose to see it.

Innocence

It takes a long time to become young.

PABLO PICASSO

Just as George Bernard Shaw once said about youth being wasted on the young, true innocence is a virtue we have to evolve into. A good working innocence is not as easy as it seems.

Often, we confuse innocence and gullibility. We would like to have the anticipation and openness of innocence and we settle for gullibility, which always gets us into trouble. Then, when we make the connection between getting in trouble and gullibility, we decide that we have to become hard and not vulnerable. We have set up a dualism of being gullible on one end and being hard and closed on the other. No wonder it takes a long time to become innocent.

We have to live long enough to know the difference between innocence and gullibility. True innocence can exist only when balanced with wisdom. Only when we have the wisdom that comes from seeing people and the world as they are can we afford the vulnerability of true innocence.

Wisdom and innocence are an unbeatable combination.

Unlearning

The first problem for all of us, men and women, is not to learn, but to unlearn.

GLORIA STEINEM

So much of our lives has been spent learning information that is either useless or dysfunctional. Very little time is spent teaching us how to live, how to take care of ourselves, how to live with one another, or how to be in touch with our feelings and know what we want and need.

We have spent so much time learning how to stuff our feelings and be out of touch with ourselves that we often experience our hearts and minds as foreign territory.

What a miracle it is that after all these years of trying to shut off our awarenesses, stuff our feelings, and be someone other than ourselves, we're still in there somewhere! We just need to peel off the learnings to find us.

When I feel like a stranger in a strange land, maybe I am. And, remember, someone must be in there feeling all this!

Rocking Chairs

Worry is like a rocking chair: it gives you
something to do but it doesn't get you anywhere.

EVAN ESAR

You know, I like rocking chairs! There is something soothing and comforting about back and forth, back and forth . . . no place to go . . . nothing to get to . . . just back and forth . . . back and forth.

Rocking in a chair is like swinging. Remember as a kid how we liked to feel the wind in our hair and the effect rocking had on our brains as we surged up and swooped back? Remember holding on to the sides of the swing, sticking our feet out and leaning back with our heads hanging and our hair falling down and out? Peaceful, wasn't it? It was as if the air and the movement cleared cobwebs and we could just hang there, suspended in space, eyes closed, not earthbound. We didn't "get anywhere" and we went somewhere.

Maybe that's the beauty of rocking chairs. They don't get anywhere by themselves, and they help us go somewhere.

Maybe if we had more rocking chairs in this world we would worry less.

Absolute Faith

The prayer that reforms the sinner and heals the sick is an absolute faith that all things are possible to God.

MARY BAKER EDDY

Mary Baker Eddy sounds old-fashioned, doesn't she? She was a great healer and a true woman of faith.

In this day and age do we ever quite believe that "all things are possible to God"? Most of us want to believe that we have some faith and that we are spiritual. Goodness knows, our politicians and our leaders keep telling us that we are a religious, spiritual nation, and "In God We Trust." But, do we really believe that God can help us lose weight? That God can work out the issues at work (in God's way—not ours, of course!)? Can we believe that a sudden death could possibly be the right thing? Do we have absolute faith?

A partial faith seems more suited to these times: Depend upon science and technology and ourselves for most things and keep God in the bullpen warming up . . . just in case.

I have known people who have had absolute faith and they were always a marvel to me. One was an old Indian Medicine Man and Spiritual Chief. He was a marvel . . . and a challenge.

Absolute faith is a possibility for all of us.

Instant Gratification

Instant gratification takes too long.
CARRIE FISHER

Now! I want it now! Fast foods ... quick fixes ... instant solutions ... complete understanding ... right now ... why can't I have it right now? ... I don't have time to wait.

We seem to have forgotten that life is a process. Everything around us is happening so fast that we are afraid we will be left in the dust if we don't have everything RIGHT NOW.

Relax, smell the flowers. We probably can't make things happen any faster and we are only putting wear and tear on ourselves by trying. We need to remind ourselves that life is a process. We are a process. And, believe it or not, both we and our lives are unfolding as we should and all we have to do is participate. We need to learn to wait with and we may have longer to wait with (live longer, that is).

Instant gratification doesn't give me time to have the experience. It may be great for machines. It leaves something to be desired in humans.

Stress

I worry more when I'm under stress.

MIA

Isn't it amazing how we put ourselves under more stress when we are already under stress? Stress has a way of turning off our perspective and drawing our brains into the fluid of anxiety. During times of stress we become flooded with waters of worry and we begin to function as if we were under water. So much energy is going into survival that we lose all perspective of what is really supportive of survival. In fact, it is almost as if our perspective is switched 180 degrees and we believe that what is bad is good for us and what is good for us we don't even see. Stress can make idiots of us all. Sometimes all we seem to be able to do is add to the stress. We need help!

Sometimes it helps just to change the setting, to take a walk somewhere we like to walk. We can still obsess while we are walking and, often, nature has a way of filling us full of perspective without our ever knowing it has happened. Or—we can do something—especially for someone else. Sometimes doing something is a good perspective shifter.

When I add to my stress, I'm not being friendly to myself.

Creating Trouble

Watch out, my dear
there's a scorpion under every stone . . .

PRAXILLA

Perhaps there is a scorpion under every rock but . . . I don't have to go around looking under rocks now, do I?

One of the most difficult realities for us humans to admit is how we create trouble for ourselves. This isn't to say that catastrophes don't just happen to us sometimes. They do. And we can learn quite a bit about ourselves and our lives when things do happen to us if we are willing to stop and look at how we contributed to the problem. Others may have contributed, too, and we may want to note that they have. And, ultimately, we are the only ones we can do anything about.

Yet, it's even more difficult to see how we actually *create* problems for ourselves when we are in our problems. It's difficult to see how we just stir the confusion or drama ever so little.

The exciting thing is that if we see we are creating problems, we can stop doing it.

A Shrinking God

*It's when I start to worry about God that I know I
have reached the ultimate level of celestial worrier.*

ANONYMOUS

One of the reasons we celestial worriers have trouble
trusting God is that we have watched our God shrink
over the years.

As children, we often had the awe of beings who
truly grasped the immensity of all creation. We were
filled with wonder and could sense the huge intercon-
nectedness that threaded around and through us. Our
childhood God could handle anything and we had trust
in that care.

Then, as we began to get older and more sophisticated, our minds took over. With minds that needed to
analyze and understand, we began to shrink our Creator
into a form and size that resembled mommies and dad-
dies, and as we grew we began to be surprised at how
closely God had come to resemble us. No wonder we
have difficulty trusting our shrunken God.

**When God is shrunken to fit what my mind can
understand and looks a lot like me, I feel insecure.**

Insulting the Creator

*The average, healthy, well-adjusted adult gets up
at seven-thirty in the morning feeling just plain
awful.*

JEAN KERR

There's some comfort in being average. At least we
won't stick out in a crowd and run the risk of being *noticed*. What a terror to be noticed. We've seen what
happens to people who get *noticed*. They get mowed
down to below everyone else's size.

People who get noticed get in trouble. Other people
don't like them and even use them for a target for their
hostility. Getting noticed can be a very scary thing,
indeed.

Yet, if being average means that we have to operate
like the rest of the world and start each morning feeling
"just plain awful," being average isn't such a great option either. What a dilemma!

We could, just in little ways, take the risk of being
ourselves now and again and see if our mornings get
better.

When I constrict myself, I insult the Creator.

Feeding Frenzy

Worriers can feed on each other just as Blue Fish feed on each other in a "Feeding Frenzy." On a trip to Boston one year I watched the Blue Fish in the Charles River in a Feeding Frenzy. They were so intent on eating that they snapped large chunks of flesh out of each other. Mortally wounding one another. They were oblivious to the fishermen who were hooking them and pulling them out of the water by the hundreds.

SHARON

So often we live our lives as if they were a feeding frenzy. We get so excited and out of touch that we find ourselves snapping at anything and everything, even if they happen to be our friends, families, or ourselves.

I had a friend who came down with a serious illness. His immediate response to his illness was to swing into action. Unfortunately, this was the response of many of his family and friends, too. People he had not seen for years were drawn by the drama of the illness and scurried around in a feeding frenzy of information. Experts from every medical center in the country were put on alert, and he was so smothered in information that he lost complete track of what decisions actually needed to be made. His friends seemed more involved in being the one to come up with the "right" answer than in finding out what he needed.

When we get into psychological feeding frenzies, we often lose great hunks of ourselves.

Hope

The only way to meet affliction is to pass through it solemnly, slowly, with humility and faith, as the Israelites passed through the sea. Then its very waves of misery will divide, and become to us a wall, on the right side and on the left, until the gulf narrows before our eyes, and we land safe on the opposite shore.

DINAH MARIA MULOCK

Hope is that spark of remembrance reminding us that whatever the previous difficulty, we got through it before. The situation may not have turned out exactly as we had hoped or as we thought it should and . . . it turned out.

Hope is that ingenious ability we have been given to shift our perspective from seeing an impossible barrier of water which could never be crossed to experiencing two protective walls of water which grant us safe passage.

Hope is that faint rising within us that moves us to open ourselves to the possibility, refusing the stuckness of assumed knowing.

Hope is a doorway. It is up to us if we choose to walk through it.

Worrying

People who tell us they are worriers say they worry anywhere from eighty to ninety-five percent of the day. It may seem that way to them, but we don't believe it's that much. By definition, people who worry more than fifty percent of the time are classified as worriers.

THOMAS PRUZINSKY

Good heavens! Are we quibbling over thirty percent here? What a wonderful example of not seeing the forest for the trees.

If worriers perceive themselves as worrying eighty to ninety-five percent of the day (assuming this is waking hours, and some report worrying in their sleep!) and the experts demand a fifty percent or above cutoff point for a clinical diagnosis, we have a problem here! Worry may be the most used legal drug in the country. Why, it would almost be un-American not to worry.

Think of the man/woman power here! Think of the potential energy being turned into kinetic energy. We could power all our major cities with worry energy! It's amazing what we will do to belong!

Yet, when we look at our willingness to spend time worrying from this perspective, we may want to reconsider.

Take a walk. Take a swim. Pick or buy some flowers. Cut down the percentages.

Wishes

May your every wish be granted.
ANCIENT CHINESE CURSE

Remember the times in our lives when we wanted everything to stay just the way it was forever? We were sure that we knew what we wanted and that was it. Lucky for us we don't have that kind of power!

We simply do not have the depth of vision or the perspective to see what will be important to us at various times and at different stages of our lives. What seemed so "right" last month may be a living horror next month.

As we move into December, we often have a tendency to start thinking in terms of wishes: what we would like, what we would like others to have. The magic of the holiday season opens up a can of worms full of romanticism and illusions if we let it. Magic, romanticism, and illusions are also fertile ground for worry if we let them be.

Maybe it's time for a reality check and time to remember that old adage: "Be careful what you ask for, you might get it!"

To have our every wish granted would, indeed, be a curse.

Decision-Making

When someone makes a decision, he is really diving into a stormy current that will carry him to places he had never dreamed of when he first made the decision.

PAULO COELHO

Life revolves around decisions—making or refusing to make them, or acting as if we are making them, or refusing to see that we have made them, or refusing to see that we are refusing to make them, or wanting someone else to make them for us so we can blame them, or pretending others have made them for us (even when they haven't!) so we can blame them. We spend a lot of time avoiding decisions.

Also, we want to make the *right* decision. We have convinced ourselves that there is such a thing as a right decision and we want to find it. The need to make decisions can generate possibilities for worry by the thousands.

Decision-making is one of our major playgrounds for growing up. It's not possible to become an adult unless we are willing to risk making decisions and to accept the consequences of our decisions.

In the final analysis, what decision we made may be far less important than having made it and accepting responsibility.

The process of making decisions and accepting responsibility for them is the door to maturity.

Elders

When a noble life has prepared for old age, it is not decline that it reveals, but the first days of immortality.

MME. DE STAËL

Sometimes our lives seem ungrounded. We seem to be swinging in space on an invisible tether that appears to be attached to nothing. No wonder we get anxious. Many of us have lost the grounding that contact with our Elders gives us. We often see our Elders as politically incorrect and technically retarded, and we cannot conceive what they have to offer us.

Native peoples the world over know that our feelings of being grounded and our ability to place ourselves meaningfully in time and space are very much related to our relationship with our Elders.

Through our Elders we experience the strings of lineage and immortality. Through them, we have the possibility of reaching beyond their lives to what they have learned from their Elders, and we can participate in the heritage of remembering.

We need our Elders.

Isolation/Alone-Time

When I worry, I reach inside and sew myself in and cut myself off to others.

BETTY

We need to learn the difference between isolation and alone-time.

Alone-time is time chosen for ourselves. Alone-time is a time we give ourselves to regroup, to wait with our inner being, and to listen to our inner process, and be receptive to that "still small voice within" when our spirituality attempts to get through to us. It is not possible to be in touch with our spirituality unless we have alone-time. Even when we are dealing with destructive or painful issues, alone-time has a feel of peace and serenity to it.

Isolation is quite different. When we go into isolation, we are not even with ourselves. We have left ourselves. Isolation is not an active choice. Isolation usually foists itself upon us and we become lost in the wanderings of our mind in a forest of fears. When we isolate, not only can other people not reach us, we cannot reach ourselves. We are lost to ourselves.

When I isolate, I need help. When I have alone-time, I have help.

Inertia/Action

The secret of getting ahead is getting started.
                              SALLY BERGER

Inertia and procrastination are often characteristics of people who worry too much. After long years of being practiced worriers, we begin to confuse worry with action. We swing back and forth from inertia and procrastination to frantic activity and give ourselves the illusion of doing something.

After our periods of frantic activity, we collapse in on ourselves and almost welcome the paralysis of worry. Clearly, both poles of this dualism support each other and perpetuate our problems even though we may have convinced ourselves we are doing something.

We need to learn to distinguish between inertia and procrastination and those moments of quiet waiting-with, when we are actively doing something about the problem. And, we need to learn to distinguish between frenetic activity and action.

When we learn these distinctions, we are on our way to healing.

Not all movement is forward.

Respecting Our Rhythms

She would not exchange her solitude for anything. Never again to be forced to move to the rhythms of others.

TILLIE OLSEN

How often have we stopped to see if our anxiety and unrest are products of our forcing ourselves to move to the rhythms of others, especially when, in that process, we have totally lost touch with our own rhythms?

Ridiculous! you say. No one can be so selfish as to just move to their own rhythms! What if everyone did that? Nothing would get done and we would have complete anarchy!

Perhaps, but would we really? When we do not respect our own rhythms, we lose touch with them and replace them with a vague feeling of uneasiness and unrest which can never quite be nailed down. When we don't respect our own rhythms, we begin to resent others and what we perceive as their impingement upon us, especially if *they* are respecting *their* own rhythms. We have forgotten how to live with ourselves and others.

Respecting our own rhythms is as important to our families and friends as it is to us.

Money in the Bank

Worry is interest paid on trouble before it is due.
WILLIAM RALPH INGE

Regardless of how good or not good we are in business matters, most of us know that to pay interest on money before it is due is foolish. A person could go broke that way!

Why, then, are we willing to pay emotional interest before it is due? When we worry, we go to our emotional bank account and draw out our reserves before they are really needed. Often we are surprised at how much reserve we have in our emotional account. If we indulge in worrying, we willingly deplete our emotional account in advance spending—of processes that pay no dividends. This behavior doesn't make much sense (cents!), does it?

When we deplete our stores, we are spent and may not have the reserves we need when we need them, except at great cost to ourselves physically and emotionally.

There are other ways of operating.

Good business and good health are related.

Humor/Despair

Humor is the sense of the Absurd which is despair refusing to take itself seriously.

ARLAND USSHER

How powerful we become when we can begin to see how absurd we are in some of our seemingly most desperate moments! When we learn to step back from ourselves and see how seriously we are taking ourselves, we have the opportunity to catch a glimpse of how *dear* we really are.

Unfortunately, we rarely stop and let ourselves see how dear we are. We can see these characteristics in others, and we tend to be a bit farsighted when it comes to seeing the "dearness" in ourselves.

Not taking ourselves too seriously is a peephole into the dearness of ourselves. It is a tiny passage that opens up into a huge cavern of ourselves, with marvelous formations formed by the dripping erosion of time far beyond our imaginations. Often, we could never have believed ourselves to have been so beautiful or intricate—partially because serious eyes tend to be myopic.

When my despair doesn't take itself so seriously, I have an opportunity to glimpse "me."

Participation

One of the great things about this job—about working at all—is that it gives me significantly less time to worry about everything.

PETE

What if worriers didn't have time to worry? What if our days held the opportunity to be so busy doing the activities and work we love to do that we just could not fit worry in? This is an interesting notion, isn't it?

When our days are full of participating in our lives and the lives of those around us, we have to struggle to fit worry in.

Perhaps worry is a luxury that has come in with leisure time, shorter work weeks, and less meaning in our lives. Our skill-training and education have not prepared us to take time for ourselves or to know what to do with it when we do.

We have learned to keep busy but do we know how to do something meaningful? We have learned to be productive but have we learned to participate in our own lives? Spirituality is, after all, participation.

It takes time and training to know what to do with ourselves when we have too much of ourselves.

Faith

Faith is an excitement and an enthusiasm; it is a condition of intellectual magnificence to which we must cling as to a treasure and not squander in . . . priggish argument.

GEORGE SAND

When it comes right down to it, we know so little about faith. We forget to remember that faith is an experience and not an idea. Whenever we try to reduce faith to a concept or an idea, it becomes lost in the verbiage. Whenever we try to generalize about faith or find an average concept that will fit everyone, we slaughter it.

Faith is individual. Faith is the myriad ways we express our uniqueness and the gifts the Creator has given us. Faith gets lost in our heads; yet, it finds its substance in our actions. We cannot really talk *about* it. We can only *do* it.

Faith is that process in all of us that leads us deep into ourselves and beyond that which we understand.

Faith is mystery in action.

The Unseen

*As we waited for the plane, Dolly told me she left
money in the car for the ride and the water. I said
I felt uncomfortable with the money being openly
viewable in the car and hoped no one needed it
badly enough to break in and take it.*

*Then I said, "But I don't have to worry—I
have insurance."*

*That's when I wondered how much of my
time, energy, spirit, and money go into "buying
trust" insurance against not having to worry.*

CONNIE

We live in a society where entire powerful industries
have evolved to "buy trust." We are willing to pay great
sums of money so we don't *have* to worry.

Worry as a way of living has become so institution-
alized that it seems woven into the warp and woof of
everyday life. Worry is certainly enmeshed in the fabric
of a society that is based upon materialism and on valu-
ing that which we can see and feel.

Maybe it's time to stop and see what's really important to us . . . the sunlight in the hair of someone we
love . . . a glimmer of excitement in a child's eye . . . the
spirit within us that connects us with all living things.

**When we are at peace with the "unseen," we have a
different perspective about the "seen."**

Hate/Resentments

*Hate is like acid. It can damage the vessel in
which it is stored as well as destroy the object
on which it is poured.*

ANN LANDERS

We tend not to think a lot about hate. We sort of have
a blanket idea that we shouldn't do it and most of us
leave it at that.

Hate seems such a strong word that it is easy to
convince ourselves that we are not really "doing that."
Yet, most of us give ourselves permission to play around
with some of its "lesser" forms, like niggling anger or resentment. Unfortunately, regardless of its forms, the effect is the same.

When we hold on to our resentments and little
treasured angers, we are indulging in feelings that are
corrosive. Resentments not only eat away at us, they
slowly and surely destroy our relationships and result in
progressive isolation.

Living in human bodies as we do, we really cannot
afford to store acid in them.

**When I see the ways I damage myself with some of my
treasured resentments, I have the option of giving
them up.**

Patience

Patience is the key to paradise.

TURKISH PROVERB

Busy people . . . important people . . . don't have much patience with patience. Patience is for old people or people who don't have responsibilities and jobs to get done. Patience is a luxury that most of us can ill afford. Patience is a luxury. Right!

Have we ever stopped and noticed how many times a day we have the opportunity to exercise patience? (Probably not—if we are impatient!) The changing of a traffic light . . . waiting for a pot to boil . . . the movements of our children in the morning . . . the process of working out a successful business deal . . . the turning of the seasons.

How often do we find ourselves lured to replace what might be opportunities to sink into the warm bath of patience with the prickles of worry?

For many of us, patience is not a natural impulse. We have to relearn it.

Patience is that process which sustains us when all else fails.

Words

*He tao rakaw, e taea te karo; he tao ki, e kore e
taea te karo.*

A wooden spear may be parried, but not the
shaft of the tongue.

MAORI PROVERB

One of the ways we can cut down our worry possibilities
is to think before we speak. Some of us have been silent
for so long that, when we finally start talking, words
tumble out of our mouths like water from a swollen
creek during the spring thaw. Others of us are so accustomed to being listened to that we have become enamored with our own voice, and we assume that anything
that tumbles out must be a grand gift that everyone de-
serves. Still others of us are so awash in pent-up feelings
that our words spurt out like a pressure cooker, letting
off steam that may have little or nothing to do with our
present circumstances.

We need to stop and recognize the power of our
words. Ultimately, it's not worth it to say something we
will have cause to worry about later or have trouble
standing behind.

*Our words reflect much more than we realize some-
times.*

Crisis/Friends

God grant me the sense of proportion to know the difference between an incident and a crisis.

ANONYMOUS

Learning to distinguish between an incident and a crisis may be one of the most important survival skills known to the human race. Worriers have a tendency to elaborate on most incidents and turn them into crises.

There are some "goodies" about crises that we might miss if we really work on this survival skill. For example, we might get less attention. When we are crisis-oriented, we tend to collect friends who are also crisis-oriented. We all gather around a crisis and feed it, regardless of whose crisis it is. "Crisis friends" might feel unsupported if we stop contributing to the "crisis" pot, and they might even get bored and move away from us.

Also, if we cut down on our crisis quotient we might miss the drama, the adrenaline, and the excitement. We might find ourselves becoming more accepting of our lives and more serene. Serenity is dull to crisis addicts.

We might even find that we enjoy just taking one step at a time and seeing what happens.

Friends who need us to be in crisis or need to be in crisis themselves really don't have much time for us, anyway.

Fooling Ourselves

When I'm trying to convince myself I'm not worrying, I am.

ANONYMOUS

Aren't we dear as human beings? We play such tricks with ourselves that we often have trouble distinguishing between the tricks we play on ourselves and our reality.

If I am trying to convince myself I am not worrying, I am. If I am trying to convince myself that I am thinking clearly and can make a good decision, I probably am not. If I am snake-oil selling myself the idea that I am feeling great, I probably don't feel so good. And, if I am assuring myself that I am feeling strong and courageous, it's a sure thing I'm not.

Did you ever stop and think how disrespectful it is to try to sell ourselves a bill of goods? Who do we think we are? Fools?!

We need to see that the way to get somewhere else is to go through where we are—not fool ourselves.

When I try to fool myself, I have a fool listening to a fool.

Nature

*Every now and again take a good look at
something not made with hands—a mountain, a
star, the turn of a stream. There will come to you
wisdom and patience and solace and, above all,
the assurance that you are not alone in the world.*

SIDNEY LOVETT

Nature is our greatest teacher. Years ago, an old American Indian Medicine Man said to me, "When you are ready come to me. I will take you into nature. There, you can learn everything you need to know."

We need time with things "not made with hands." Regardless of who or where we are, nature, in some form, is accessible to us. We may only have a plant in our living room, the glimpse of a winter sky, or a lone tree in stark silhouette against the skyline, and nature is always there. We are the ones who go away . . . nature never goes away.

Nature returns me to the part of myself that can never get lost.

Reality Testing

All the beautiful sentiments in the world weigh less than a single lovely action.

JAMES RUSSELL LOWELL

Our worries would be halved if we could only learn to focus not on what others say but on what they do. Even people who mean well toward us are often confused about what is really true for them. Often, people who care about us really *want* to do what they say they will, and they just don't quite make it. Or, somewhere, their thoughts and ambitions are just greater than their abilities. Or, maybe they are living lives that just don't let them be the kind of friends they want to be.

We can start to realize that we have all the information we need to see what's really going on with those around us. We lose touch with our perspective and information when we let ourselves buy into the illusions others live with and by. When we let ourselves use the information we have about those we love and accept them as they are—even if we don't like the way they are—we have less grief.

Look at the action, not the words. Believe the action.

Humor

*Humor is an affirmation of dignity, a declaration
of man's superiority to all that befalls him.*

ROMAIN GARY

That we can still laugh is a testament to us all. Often, it
seems, those who have the greatest ability to laugh at
themselves are those who have been through the most.
Life has softened them up a bit.

How often have we thought of humor as an affirmation of our dignity? When we make a faux pas and
everyone around us laughs with us, can we see that as an
affirmation of dignity? If not, we're probably taking life
and ourselves too seriously.

When someone lovingly teases us about the pie on
our tie, can we see that as an affirmation of dignity? If
not, we're probably on the verge of becoming terminally
serious.

When tension is high and someone cracks a joke,
can we see that as affirming human dignity? If not, we
are probably a drain on the team.

Humor is multidimensionality briefly squeezed into
linear time and space.

**Those of us who still take life seriously probably
haven't "got" it yet.**

Rocking the Boat

The eighth deadly sin is to rock the boat.

SANDRA CONEY

One of the greatest wastes of expenditures of time and energy is time spent in trying not to "rock the boat." For one thing, it's almost impossible to be alive and not rock the boat. Babies rock the boat, don't they? They come in kicking and screaming and not only ask us to meet their needs, they ask us to completely rearrange our lives while doing it. Real live babies have a way of shoving the boat off the shore into rapids that other parents have kept secret from us.

Growth rocks the boat, doesn't it? How upset we get when a spouse or family member grows and changes and doesn't warn us about it beforehand!

Life rocks the boat, doesn't it? Just when we thought the purpose of life was to get everything the way we wanted it and keep it that way . . . plans change . . . people change . . . life changes.

Only dead women and men can be expected not to rock the boat, and even they surprise us, at times.

Love

The truth is—worry deadens love.

SUE WHITAKER

Love is one of the most enduring and, at the same time, most delicate of human emotions. In some ways love is like energy—it can neither be created nor destroyed, and it can be changed.

We have so many confusions about love that it is exceedingly difficult just to let it be. Most of us desperately believe that we want love and we are constantly looking for "more, better, faster." How much pain we feel when we realize that often our most sincere attempts, such as worrying, not only deaden our own love, they also deaden feelings of love in those whom we are trying to love.

When love begins to deaden, we feel even more desperate and try to control it even more, which often results in even more isolation and fear.

When we can just relax and remember that love is a flow of energy between people—a gift that can neither be controlled nor created—then, we may be on our way.

Love is a gift that happens when we let go of everything we thought worked.

Anticipation

Tain't worthwhile to wear a day all out before it comes.

SARAH ORNE JEWETT

Days that aren't here yet aren't here yet. Sounds simple, doesn't it? It is! There is no way we can make a day get here before it does. We worriers only think of anticipation in negative terms, and wear ourselves and the day out in the process.

Anticipation can be fun, too. There is no time like the holiday season to let ourselves remember excited anticipation. Remember the decorated department store windows and how we were huddled up to go see them as kids? Even though the holiday season starts earlier and earlier we can still have the immediate thrill of anticipation. We can be excited about our gifts and those we are giving, and let anticipation go at that. We can dip into magic and get simple with the miracle of the new day.

The content of my anticipation is up to me.

Feelings

If I knew what I was so anxious about, I wouldn't be so anxious.

MIGNON MCLAUGHLIN

Part of the human condition is that sometimes we just feel anxious. We don't know *what* we are anxious about; we just are anxious. Being human, we launch into trying to find out *what* we are anxious about, because we have deluded ourselves into believing that if we understand our anxiety we can then figure the problem out, and we'll either be all right or we can worry about it.

How disrespectful this process is of ourselves! When we are anxious, we are anxious. The anxiety usually isn't there for no reason. If we let ourselves sit with the feeling and not run from it, often we can move to a new level of working it through that is beyond our brains.

We can begin to see that anxiety isn't an attack, it is a gift of understanding in our being, not just in our minds.

Feelings are not my enemies. What I do with them is up to me.

Seasons

You got to grab while you can or it might be gone.

MAN IN ELEVATOR

Remember when we were younger and we bought something we really loved to wear, and then next month or even next year we could go back and get another one of the same thing just because we loved it so much?

We have adjusted to planned obsolescence and a consumer society with knee-jerk responses that encourage us to grab whatever we can whenever we can and run. What if we miss our big opportunity?

Thankfully, this season gives us the opportunity to shift gears and slow down a little bit. We have the opportunity to unpack old treasures and tenderly touch and feel them. We have the opportunity to pull out the old boxes, unwrap the newspaper, or the worn tissue paper, and exclaim, "I remember that one!"

We see dishes, silverware, and platters that have been sleeping encased in their protective coverings. We can take the time to remember and for at least a few days, we don't have to grab and run.

The seasons give us varieties of rememberings.

Guidance

*There is a guidance for each of us, and by lowly
listening we shall hear the right word.*

RALPH WALDO EMERSON

Have we become too sophisticated to believe that each
of our lives is guided? Let's hope not.

The issue may not be the lack of guidance. The issue may be that we have forgotten how to listen.

We look to experts who write "how-to" or "self-
help" books and search the bookstores and the TV
channels for someone who knows more about ourselves
than we do.

We plunge into research and believe that if we can
just read enough studies, especially the "definitive"
study, we will have an answer. We want someone, anyone, to tell us what to do, thus relieving us of the
responsibility for our lives.

There is absolutely nothing wrong with information, even if we gather it in a strange way. Our real
problem comes when we do not take the time to sit
with our guidance and give in to "lowly listening," as
long as it takes.

**When I listen to my guidance running through me, I
get great "advice."**

Spaces

Anxiety is the space between the "now" and the "then."

RICHARD ABELL

Filling spaces can become a major pastime. What is it in us that avoids a void?

Zen Masters teach us to focus upon our breathing and simply to become aware of it. As we become aware of our breathing, we come to realize that our breath does not just go in-out, in-out. Our awareness leads us into the realization that if we let our bodies do the breathing for us, there is a space between inhale and exhale and between exhale and inhale. Most of us are rarely aware of our breathing at all, thanks to the autonomic nervous system and, if we are aware, rarely do we let ourselves focus on the spaces. As we let our awareness light upon the spaces, we come to realize that there is a lot going on "between."

When we resist the urge to fill in voids and spaces, we begin to know that our most important moments may be the "betweens."

Betweens take courage.

Chatter

Gossip isn't scandal and it's not merely malicious. It's chatter about the human race by lovers of the same.

PHYLLIS MCGINLEY

Chatter can be a lovely and a loving activity. There is nothing warmer than two old friends "catching up." "Chatter about the human race by lovers of the same" is a tried and true way for new friends to get to know one another.

Chatter during the holidays is a way to catch up and check in. It is an information network and a broadcast system all wrapped up in one.

When we realize that it is none of our business what others say about us, we can stop and let ourselves realize that if people are gossiping about us, we must mean something to them. At the very least, they are spending some time with us!

When I let myself realize that if I want to gossip about someone, that person must have some importance to me, and maybe I can let myself feel what's under my desire to gossip and . . . I may be surprised.

Loving chatter is never a waste of time.

Simplicity

Do what you can, with what you have, where
you are.

THEODORE ROOSEVELT

Simple, isn't it? Doing what we can, with what we have, where we are, sort of sums it up, doesn't it?

As the year draws to a close, some of us may want to take advantage of the ending of the old year to make a "beat ourselves up" list. We easily focus on the goals we haven't reached, the dreams unfulfilled, and tasks uncompleted.

Where did we learn to be so hard on ourselves? Perfectionism has slowly crept into our psyches, and we have lost the tenderness of acceptance.

Life is really quite simple, you know. We truly can only do what we can, with what we have, where we are. To ask anything more of ourselves would be unrealistic and idiotic.

Simplicity may save me from idiocy.

Finding Our Way Home

Yes, I have doubted. I have wandered off the path. I have been lost. But I always returned. It is beyond the logic I seek. It is intuitive—an intrinsic, built-in sense of direction. I seem to find my way home. My faith has wavered but has saved me.

HELEN HAYES

Wandering off our path can take many forms. So many opportunities arise to challenge our integrity. Friends need help on their doctorates and we do the work and let them claim it as their own. This doesn't hurt us. After all, they were the ones who compromised their honesty . . . or were they?

We get angry and upset with someone who acts like an idiot toward us, and we allow ourselves to believe that we are justified in acting the same way.

We were later than we said we were because there was no one there to check and we let our colleagues apologize for being late.

It's so easy to slip off the path, isn't it? Yet, it's comforting to know the path is always there.

Peace

We should have much peace if we would not busy ourselves with the sayings and doings of others.

THOMAS À KEMPIS

Peace would be easy if we were all alone and practiced the life of a hermit or a monk. In day-to-day life, peace is often in short supply.

Perhaps this would be a good day to stop and take stock and see the little ways we rob ourselves of the peacefulness of ordinary living.

Do we create a crisis when all we are dealing with is living?

Do we expect more of ourselves than could be expected from any human being and then beat ourselves up when we don't meet our expectations?

Do we focus outside ourselves not to be of service but to obsess over what others are saying and doing?

Do we fail to stop when we need to stop because we really don't believe we have a right to stop?

Who needs a jailer when we have ourselves?

Miracles

Be realistic. Expect a miracle.

IAN GROWLER

The above statement was made by an Australian man who was filled with cancerous tumors and given only a short while to live. That prediction was given to him by the medical profession many years ago.

We are always impressed with these stories of miracles and often choose to see miracles as the exception and not the rule.

We divide up our thinking into three categories—optimism, pessimism, and realism—and unconsciously have equated pessimism and realism, studiously avoiding the negative label of being an (ugh) optimist.

But, wait a minute! How easily we forget the everydayness of miracles!

A hurricane changes direction, missing all land masses and heading out to sea. A baby survives a car crash where all others were killed.

A flower blooms. A bird sings. A river flows. The sun rises—again.

Miracles are everyday. Miracles are realistic.

Index

Anne Wilson Schaef, Ph.D., is a world-renowned writer, lecturer, and teacher. She has pioneered a new approach to healing called Living In Process, which she teaches throughout the world. Living In Process is a way of being fully alive while participating fully in a new paradigm. She is the author of the bestselling *Meditations for Women Who Do Too Much* and numerous other books that have been translated worldwide. Her books have been described as provocative, spiritual, and healing.